The Battle for Transportation Supremacy

The Battle for Transportation Supremacy

How the Titans of Transportation Positioned Their Companies over the Past 170 Years in the Boston to New York Corridor

Lawrence Walsh

THE BATTLE FOR TRANSPORTATION SUPREMACY
HOW THE TITANS OF TRANSPORTATION POSITIONED THEIR COMPANIES OVER THE PAST 170 YEARS IN THE BOSTON TO NEW YORK CORRIDOR

Cover photo of New York, New Haven and Hartford Railroad Co. logo courtesy of New Haven Railroad Historical & Technical Association, Inc.

Cover photo of Archibald Angus McLeod courtesy of VIADUCTgreene Organization

iUniverse books may be ordered through booksellers or by contacting:

iUniverse LLC
1663 Liberty Drive
Bloomington, IN 47403
www.iuniverse.com
1-800-Authors (1-800-288-4677)

ISBN: 978-1-4917-2738-6 (sc)
ISBN: 978-1-4917-2740-9 (hc)
ISBN: 978-1-4917-2739-3 (e)

Library of Congress Control Number: 2014904183

Printed in the United States of America.

iUniverse rev. date: 06/30/2014

Contents

Illustrations

Acknowledgments

This work began about fifteen years ago. At first I was intrigued by a comment of a lifelong friend and a resident of Springfield, Massachusetts, named John R. Lynch. Why had the Inland Route (Springfield Line) become the orphan in the Boston–New York travel market? At its inception in the 1860s, the Inland Route was favored over the Shore Line. It reached the most populous intermediate points, provided fast time, and required no change of seats en route. Now some 150 years later the Inland Route is but a memory.

As the work evolved, some of my associates at the San Diego Model Railroad Club and the Longhorn Chapter of the National Railway Historical Society wanted the facts about that expensive seven-mile line formed in 1912 and called the New York Connecting Railroad. Its crown jewel is the Hell Gate Bridge. My inquirers wanted to know why this structure has been singularly underutilized for most of its ninety-five years.

The late Ray Baxter, friend, author, and alumnus of Harsimus Cove duties on the Pennsylvania Railroad and the adjoining Erie Railroad, was generous with his time and read drafts of this work, thereby providing valuable comments and direction. So did Paul Hart of the Lackawanna Chapter of the National Railway Historical Society and Matt Walsh, author and proponent of *The New Urbanism* and *Transit Villages*.

I am most grateful to Patricia Mitchell, a journalism major who read and marked up an earlier draft of this work. Patricia has a way of making my words sound more graceful. Marguerite Walsh read the manuscript and shared with me her thoughts on how to inject a bit more punch and clarity into my word selection. Her comments are most gratefully received. I also thank Laura K. Smith, curator for Business, Railroad and Labor Collections, who patiently guided me through her splendidly maintained collection at the University of Connecticut Libraries at Storrs. Special thanks for the use of splendid photos go to William Dulmaine of the New Haven Railroad Historical & Technical Association, Inc., Jim Roache of the Canton Historical Society, Jeff Edwards, Scott Ives of Currier & Ives, Vinny Devine of Igor I. Sikorsky Historical Archives, and Paul vanMeter of the VIADUCTgreene organization. Finally I bow in admiration of J. W. Swanberg and his publication *New Haven Power* (1838–1968). He must have spent years in accumulating the data and pictures and publishing it in an easy-to-understand taxonomy. His work is a gem and must have been driven by his own love of the subject.

Most of all I am grateful to my wife, Hilda M., for her willingness to read and reread drafts of the work and her continuous and upbeat signals for me to keep rewriting where further improvements can be made. Her unflagging enthusiasm has been my driving force.

Lawrence A. Walsh
San Antonio, TX, 2012

September 2013 Update:

I faced two major setbacks in this period plus one major gain.

My first setback was the loss of my dear wife and faithful friend, Hilda. Then there followed a major health setback for me. I awoke one morning and found that my walk and my talk were not working. I was moved to a therapy center but remained unable to walk or talk much. I am a bedridden invalid, yet with a clear mind. As I lay in my bed of sorrow, I wondered, *Is this the end of fifteen years' work? Who in the family might be ready and able to become our executive editor?*

Surprise! A family member did step forward. Marguerite (Cookie) Walsh would take the job. With the aid of a part-time associate, she is on the job! Fortunately the writing is done and most illustrations are in hand, some still awaiting approval. Will the work be ready for the publisher in 2014? I believe so.

My work has been rescued by a daughter-in-law. And life goes on. How strange and wonderful.

The Boston to New York Rail Lines and 170 Years of Struggle

- how they planned their strategies
- how they chose their supporting tactics and why
- the successes they experienced
- the failures they confronted
- what they learned from these battles for supremacy

The Titans

- Samuel Rea
- Alexander J. Cassatt
- J. P. Morgan
- William Henry Vanderbilt I
- Chauncey Mitchell Depew
- Archibald Angus McLeod

Introduction

Boston and New York, two major eastern seaboard cities, are just 230 miles apart. Connecting the two with good transportation has been the goal of rival transportation companies for more than two hundred years. Railroads have been in the thick of this struggle for market share almost from their beginnings in 1834.

The relatively short distance between the two cities would seem to suit and even favor rail travel. Indeed, from their humble beginnings in 1834, the rail companies did gain share until by 1916 they were the dominant means of travel using either public or private transportation. In these growth years, the railroad companies were fat and happy. Their "widows and orphans" stock was considered gilt edge. They felt their competitors were other railroad companies serving the same market and, to a lesser extent, the steamship companies. But by 1920 the rail companies realized they had new competition from the automobile. By 1940 another competitor appeared in the form of commercial aviation. As more years rolled by, the railroad hegemony disappeared. In the 1950s the automobile thrived as the new interstate highway system was put in place. In the early 1960s commercial aviation introduced the Boston–New York Air Shuttle that threatened rail management right down to its very existence.

In the late 1960s the federal Department of Transportation, perhaps recognizing its largesse to highways and commercial aviation, had tilted the playing field against the railroads, decided to throw two bones out to northeast rail companies. Both were dubbed demonstration projects, presumably to demonstrate whether rail had any future at all in the northeast corridor. The first demonstration introduced special high-speed, multiple-unit electric cars to be named Metroliners. These cars would serve the New York–Washington, DC, market—225 miles apart. Because the northern segment of the northeast corridor lacked complete electrification, the Department of Transportation ordered two Turbotrains, specially built by United Technologies, to race over the Boston–New York segment of the northeast corridor. By 1977, an evaluation of the two demonstrations showed the Washington–New York Metroliners were a success. The two Turbotrains were a flop.

By the mid–1970s the outlook for Boston–New York rail market looked dismal. The New Haven Railroad, dominant manager of the Boston–New York rail lines, had gone out of business. In 1969 it was merged into a reluctant Penn Central Railroad, itself not far from bankruptcy. In 1971 Congress established Amtrak, a federal entity to relieve troubled freight railroads of their passenger service obligations. In 1976 another federal entity called Conrail was established to rescue from bankruptcy the Penn Central Railroad (and other eastern roads) and to assure rail freight operations would continue. Was the end of passenger rail near?

Somewhat miraculously, by 2002 an almost-moribund Boston–New York rail corridor had sprung back as a competitor for market share. The entire line was electrified, and high-speed "bullet" trains called Acela Expresses were racing between the end points at unheard-of speeds of 150 miles per hour and in a less impressive end-point time of three and one-half hours. Will the Acela Express trains earn a return on their public investment?

The financial ups and downs of the Boston–New York rail lines make an interesting study of how rail management down through the decades responded to the challenges. This book outlines the environment, the corporate decisions, and the consequences of 170 years of rail operations. The Monday morning quarterback always has the advantage. It is still instructive to analyze each situation, the available options, and the consequences of decisions.

There once was a substantial amount of rail freight traffic in the Boston–New York corridor, most of which is now gone. This loss made passenger traffic decisions more difficult, but the full reasons why rail freight traffic was all but lost are beyond the scope of this work. We are concerned chiefly about market share in the passenger market. Thus, we will use fourteen different years, stretching from pre-rail 1800 to 2010 in order to look in on operations. The public passenger timetables published for these look-in years provide unmistakable evidence of how rail management responded to its challenges down through the years.

Moving the rail line and its trains from the private sector to the public sector has changed the rules of the game. While in the private sector railroad companies have an insistent mandate to earn a profit or go out of business, in the public sector the mandate is less clear. In the political world of government control there is a still unsettled dispute over whether passenger rail is needed and should be subsidized at all. If so, what performance indicators should be used to judge the success or failure of such government-controlled operations?

This work concludes with the unfolding story of Amtrak's Acela train. Is the Acela Express in the Boston–New York City market important? Probably it is. To date there has been but one model of success in attracting a substantial share of people choosing to ride together between end points rather than using other forms of public transportation or their own personal transportation. The "riding together" model applies mainly to distances of from two to three hundred miles and excludes purely commuter train operations. That success model has been the New York City and Washington, DC, market where Amtrak's moderately high-speed trains (Metroliners and Acelas) have reportedly captured up to 60 percent of the total market as defined above.

If Boston–New York City can show a similar success, perhaps capturing at least 30 percent of the total market, then a second success model is here to confirm the first model.

To be sure, there are a number of moderate-speed rail passenger corridors currently operating over freight railroads. The corridors are largely state-supported and -funded, such as California's Pacific Surfliner Route, the Capital Corridor, and the San Joaquins. Each of these has enjoyed impressive ridership growth. So has the Pacific Northwest's Cascade Corridor or the New York City–Albany Empire Corridor or the New York-to-Harrisburg Keystone Corridor. Still, none of these moderate-speed corridors has achieved the travel diversion and dominance enjoyed by the New York City and Washington, DC,

Corridor. What would it take to make the above corridors a dominant success?

Further, what would it take to activate potential corridors that do not now exist—corridors such as the Texas Triangle (Houston–Dallas, Dallas–San Antonio, and San Antonio–Houston)? We believe it will take several success models aided and abetted by growing traffic congestion and relatively high gasoline prices. Where will the political leadership come from? Rail passenger service in the United States has seen a good deal of indifference or outright hostility from presidential administrations for at least seventy-five years (with the notable exception of the Obama administration). Don't wait for the politicos to initiate action. Do join the people who feel the pressure for an attractive travel alternative, do observe what peoples of many other countries are enjoying, and do demand equal service here at home.

Chapter 1: 1800

Just before the Railroad

Since no passenger railroads existed in 1800, why use this as a look-in year? I do so mainly to observe the abysmal travel conditions that prevailed between the two great seaports—New York and Boston. This will help explain why, when the railroad finally arrived, the early, erratic, unpredictable performance of rail travel was tolerated and why for all their shortcomings the early railroads were received so warmly.

In the year 1800, President John Adams was barely in the brand-new White House in the equally new federal capital of Washington, DC. The three great seaports of the new nation were Boston, New York, and Philadelphia. Painful as it was, travel between Boston and New York, the two end points of our study, was sometimes essential.

Departing from Boston, travelers had four choices. They could take the all sea route (illustration 1-1), boarding their sailing ship in Boston Harbor. From there, it was out into the open ocean, around Cape Cod, and on to New York via Long Island Sound or via the open ocean south of Long Island all the way to the New York harbor. The sound route was shorter and preferred, but the all-ocean route had fewer navigational hazards and was free of an enemy attack from the shore as in the War of 1812. The sailing ships were cramped. The food was poor. Timekeeping was erratic, subject to wind and tide. Trip time could be two weeks as likely as one week.

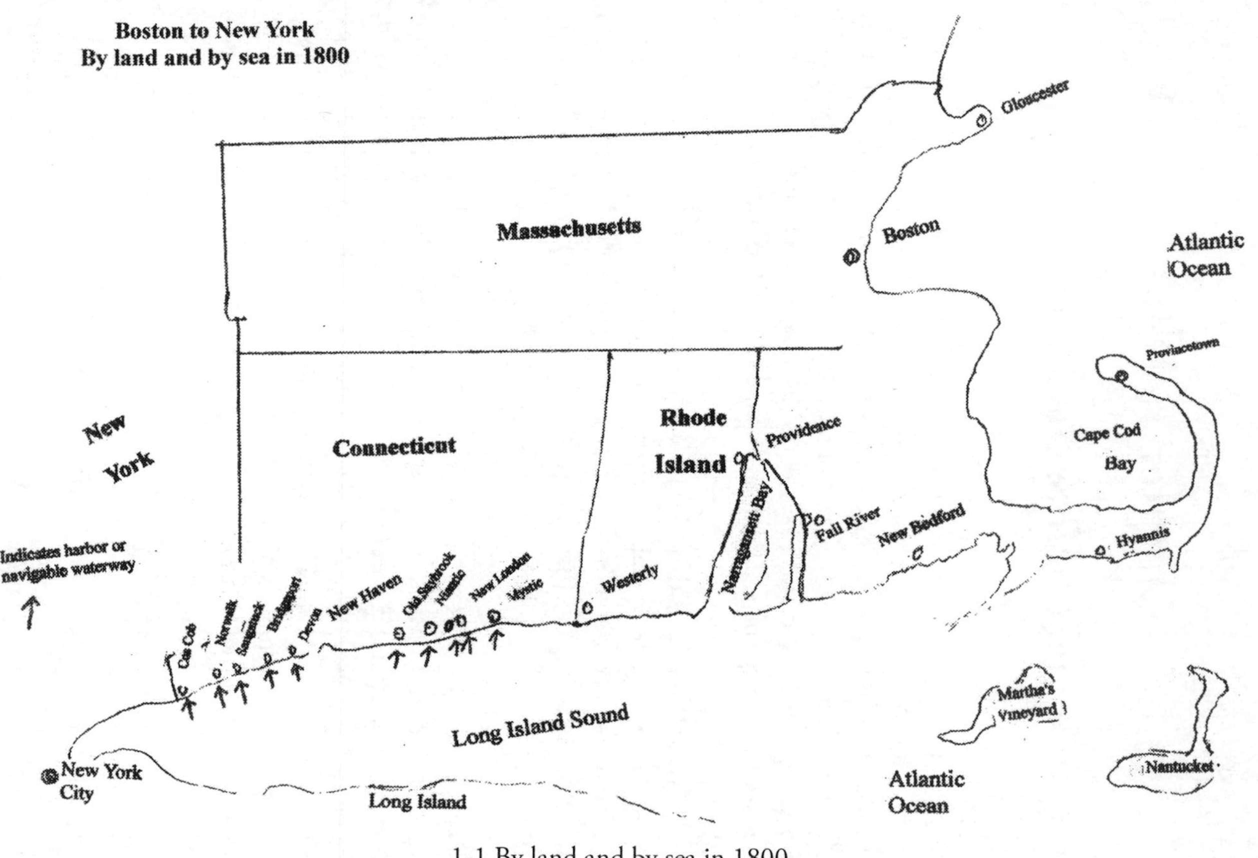
Boston to New York
By land and by sea in 1800
Gloucester
Massachusetts
Boston
Atlantic Ocean
Provincetown
Cape Cod Bay
New York
Connecticut
Rhode Island
Providence
Narragansett Bay
Fall River
New Bedford
Hyannis
Indicates harbor or navigable waterway
Cos Cob
Norwalk
Saugatuck
Bridgeport
Devon
New Haven
Old Saybrook
Niantic
New London
Mystic
Westerly
Martha's Vineyard
Long Island Sound
New York City
Long Island
Atlantic Ocean
Nantucket

1-1 By land and by sea in 1800

A second choice was to use a stagecoach (illustrations 1-2a, b). The roads were primitive. The ride was uncomfortable. Trip time varied from one week on nice, warm summer days with long hours of daylight to more than two weeks on short, cold, dark winter days. Stagecoach travelers could look forward to a warm post house or wayside tavern each evening where food, drink, and a bed awaited.

1-2a Butterfield Stage Coach
Courtesy of the Jeff Edwards Collection, Porterville, California

1-2b Stage coach en route from Porterville to Hot Springs, California
Courtesy of the Jeff Edwards Collection, Porterville, California

A third choice was to combine the above two options. By taking the stagecoach down the forty-four miles to Providence to board a sailing ship there, several travel days could be saved. This still left a total trip time of a week or longer.

Finally the traveler could use personal transportation, much as John Adams did on his journey to the Second Continental Congress in 1776. He and his traveling companion, Joseph Bass, saddled their horses and strapped on their belongings.[1] The traveler had to be in a fairly vigorous condition, even given the comfort of the coach stops. The Boston–New York trip time by horse could be as little as five days in warm weather or longer than ten days in frigid weather with consequent delays at ice-choked ferry crossings.

There simply was no good, simple, comfortable, and reliable way to make the journey. The trip, which is routine today, was an adventure then.

---

1 David G. McCullough, *John Adams* (New York, NY: Simon and Schuster, 2001).

Chapter 2: 1834–1845

Getting Started, Experiments Lead to Success

In 1804 James Watt first harnessed the power of steam with a tiny stationary engine. To the entrepreneurs of the day, multiple possible uses came to mind. The engine could be used to move belts and pulleys attached by gears to the constantly rotating cam gear of the engine. The belts and pulleys could be attached and detached at will. The owners of gristmills and textile mills seized on the invention, reducing their dependence on waterpower. Canal builders found the stationary steam engines could lift boats up or down dry inclines fitted with guideways, reducing their dependence on sluices, flumes, and locks.

Operators of horse-drawn railroads could lift heavily laden cars up steep gradients by using a chain attached to boat and steam engine. Cars could return on the same route by lowering them down via engine and cable, or they could be rolled back to their downhill origin via a separately graded "gravity" railroad.

The owners of small sailing vessels, eager to eliminate their dependence on wind and sails, brought the stationary steam engine right on board their ships for the purpose of powering paddle wheels for propulsion. The early steam ships were little more than river ferries. But by 1835 steam ship owners were emboldened enough to build ships such as the *Lexington* for service on Long Island Sound, shuttling between Providence, Rhode Island, and New York City. These ships carried no backup sails (illustration 2-1).

2-1 Steamship Lexington
"Awful Conflagration of the Steamboat Lexington" published by Nathaniel Currier 1840, courtesy of Scott Currier of Currier & Ives

The steamship *Lexington* was commissioned in 1835 by none other than Cornelius Vanderbilt, the commodore and dominant member of the shipping industry. Indeed the *Lexington* was to be no ordinary addition to Vanderbilt's fleet of boats. Rather, this was to be the ship that dared to sail in open waters without sails. Up to this time, about the only way sails could be dispensed with would have been a short ferry-type crossing. The newness and vagaries of motorized propulsion without a single backup sail was considered reckless. The *Lexington* was to be the proof that the time for exclusive dependence on motorized propulsion had arrived.

> The first five years after its launching was when the *Lexington* would prove its worth. Not dependent on winds and tide, the ship set the speed records for travel between Boston and New York, initially via Providence, Rhode Island, and later via Stonington, Connecticut, with rail completing the trip in both cases. For its time, the ship was large, with a 207-foot length and a weight of 488 gross tons, including its side wheels. Even with about 175 crew and passengers aboard plus 150 bales of cotton, the ship was roomy with space for an elementary dining room, which was previously unheard of.
>
> Alas, a tragic fire would overwhelm and sink the ship and take 139 of the 143 lives aboard. The fire occurred on the evening of January 14, 1840. This might have delayed any further immediate development of mechanical propulsion, but this did not happen. Although this disaster occurred almost two hundred years ago, it remains to this day Long Island Sound's worst steamboat loss. But an inquest jury did not blame the mechanical propulsion as such. Rather, it blamed a series of fatal design flaws. The ship's boilers had originally been built to burn wood but had been converted to coal in 1839. This conversion had not been properly completed. Not only does coal burn hotter that wood, but extra coal was being burned on the night of the fire because of rough seas. A spark from the overheated smokestack set the stack's casing ablaze on the freight deck. The fire spread to the bales of cotton, which were stored improperly close to the stack. Further, the crew was inept in properly launching the three lifeboats, causing all three to fail and sink.

Could not the steam engine be mounted on and propel a land vehicle? A steam-powered road coach would offer too much friction and too little stability. But what of a rail-mounted vehicle? By 1829, 1830, and 1831, several experimental locomotives with upright boilers were mounted on a platform with flanged iron wheels to roll along a fixed guideway. (Illustrations 2-2a and b show Tom Thumb with an upright boiler and the Dewitt Clinton with a horizontal boiler.) These experimental teakettles worked (sort of), being able to pull one or several coaches. It was enough for the Commonwealth of Massachusetts to issue three charters in 1830 and 1831 for proposed rail lines to radiate out from the hub city of Boston. One was the Boston and Worcester Railroad, which commenced service in 1834 over the forty-four-mile route between its namesake cities. Another was the Boston and Providence Railroad, also a forty-four-miler bridging the gap between its namesake cities in 1835. Two of the Boston–New York rail lines had made a beginning.

2-2 Five very early steam engines, 1829

The Dewitt Clinton

The John Bull, 1831
Smithsonian Collection

Tom Thumb, 1829

Stourbridge Lion, 1829
Smithsonian Collection

The decade between 1835 and 1845 were the infant years of the Boston–New York rail lines. Although mother country England provided a few prototypes, trial and error was the rule. The public was generally quite accepting of this, including the investors. Before 1845 arrived, the belts and gears that drove the earliest engines gave way to machines with horizontal boilers, steam chests exhausting steam against reciprocating pistons, in turn connected to drive rods and the locomotive drive wheels. Once vertical boilers went horizontal, steam locomotives were classified by their wheel arrangement. The front-leading wheels were known as pilots or ponies. They guided the engine through curves, gave it stability, and supported the weight of the steam cylinders and smoke box. The larger rear sets of wheels were the drivers and supported the locomotive's main weight.

Fig. 7. American Type.

2-3 A 4-4-0 American-type steam engine
A winner!

By 1845, our look-in year, vertical boilers and six-wheelers were passé. In 1836 Henry Roe Campbell patented the 4-4-0 American-type engine. It would become the standard engine for passenger travel (and some freight service too) for the next sixty years. With four drive wheels and four pony wheels, it was stable. It rode well, and it could pull four or five small wooden cars.

With the teething pains of the locomotive put to rest, what of the roadbed and the cars? The railroad builders of 1830 to 1835 tried to lay track on wooden ties and on granite blocks. The granite blocks were very stable and lasted forever but were pricey. Wood won out. The wood ties would rot out in ten years or less given the poor drainage, lack of ballast, and primitive wood preservatives in use. Wood was the early favorite for the rails too. They were affixed directly to the wood ties. To avoid premature wear and splintering, iron strap rail was secured to the top of the wooden guideway. Since the iron strap rail was delivered to the railroad in coils, strap rail was always under some tension when nailed to the wood. Strap rail had the annoying tendency to come loose as the cars bounced over the nail head. Being under tension, the suddenly loose strap rail would snake right through the floorboards of a carriage, frightening and endangering its occupants. By 1845 this snaking problem was solved by installing solid iron T rail.

The passenger carriages themselves evolved. To get started, many rail companies simply took road carriages and fitted them with flanged iron wheels. By 1845 these had given way to carriages designed for railway use. These cars were wooden except for wheels and draft gear. They initially had one axle under each end, which grew to two axles by 1845. They loaded at their ends through open platforms, had flat roofs, windows, and, glory be, a wood stove for some heat. By 1845 the wildest of the trial and errors were over. The infant railroad had grown into a youngster with growing credibility and acceptance. Just where was this youngster headed?

Expansion

Illustration 2-4 shows how far the rail lines of 1845 had progressed as they inched forward between Boston and New York. It was possible to ride west out of Boston over three contiguous railroads and reach New Haven, Connecticut, via Worcester, Springfield, and Hartford, via the Inland Route. It was also possible to travel west out of Boston on the Shore Line all the way to Stonington, Connecticut, by using two railroads and bridging a short rail gap in Providence by coach.

By 1845, the outlines of the Inland route and the Shoreline route were beginning to take form

No moveable span bridges were required between Boston and Stonington, or between Boston, Springfield and New Haven.

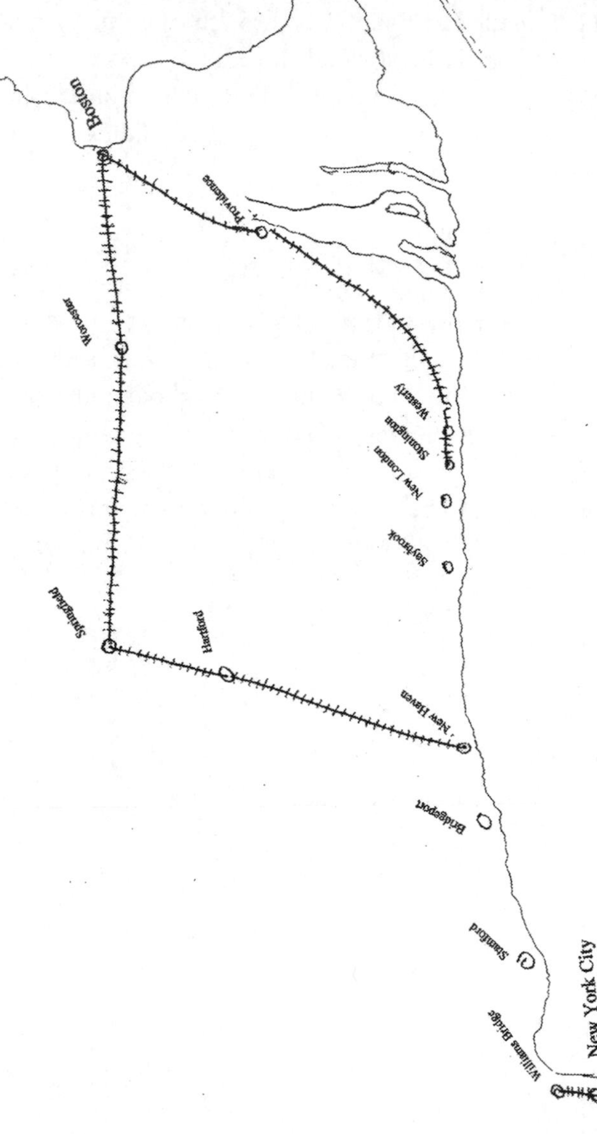

2-4 Route outlines taking form in 1845

The owners of the new steamship companies welcomed these early railroads. To Cornelius Vanderbilt and other steamship owners, the railroad eased travel between Boston and New York. Their owners were uncomfortable allowing their ships to venture into the open ocean around Cape Cod and the eastern embarking ports of Providence, Stonington, and New Haven since there were no backup sails in case of engine failure while people were traversing the open ocean part of the voyage. The rail ride to Providence, for example, was down to three hours. By transferring to the steamship in Providence, the traveler could move between Boston and New York in just under one full day. Compared to the sailing ships, the steamers were relatively comfortable and commodious, even offering a rudimentary dining room. My, what a contrast with just forty-five years ago!

In 1845 a novel but short-lived Boston–New York route surfaced. This journey would require three rail lines and two steamships. The route was from Boston to Providence, thence by another rail company from Providence to Stonington, Connecticut. At Stonington a steamer took the traveler across Long Island Sound to Greenport, Long Island, where the cars of the newly completed Long Island Railroad were boarded. The Long Island Railroad deposited the traveler at the Fulton Street ferry in Brooklyn, whence by the final steamship across the East River to Manhattan Island, New York City.

The rail gap between Boston and New York was closing on the west end too. The New York and Harlem Railroad had established a station at Twenty-Third Street and Park Avenue in the city. From there it headed due north up Park Avenue, bridged the Harlem River, entered what is now the borough of the Bronx, and went on up to White Plains via Williams Bridge (where a junction, later to be called Woodlawn, would be established with the Boston lines).

2-5 Some early steam motives in S-scale

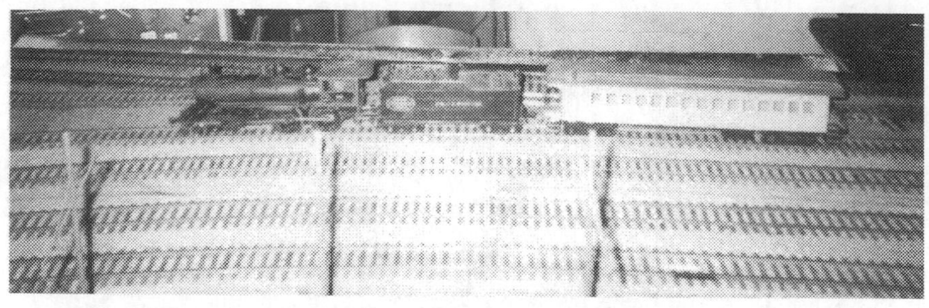

It's 1868 in miniature at the San Diego Model Railroad Club. A 4-4-0 American type locomotive is steamed up and ready to haul an open-platform, clerestory-roofed car down the Inland Route.

It's 1915 in miniature and a 4-6-2 "Pacific" is steaming up at the roundhouse. Author's collection

That 124-Mile Gap between Williams Bridge and Stonington

In 1845 the lack of a rail line connecting Williams Bridge and New Haven (sixty miles) and New Haven and Stonington (sixty-four miles) had little to do with a lack of interest and everything to do with a lack of technology. Getting over ravines and unnavigable waterways was no problem for the early railroads. Wooden trestles and even immense stone masonry arches were used to bridge such areas. The Canton Viaduct (illustration 2-6) shows what civil engineers could do in 1835. Getting across *navigable* waterways was another matter. Here a movable bridge was required. Molded or cast iron that was used in early bridgework was brittle and lacked tensile strength, limiting the weight of engines they could accommodate. By 1845 wrought iron came into use. It was a purified form of iron that was more easily shaped, formed, and welded. For a bridge that had to swing open and shut for navigation, structural engineers never felt very comfortable about the safety of cast iron.

2-6 The Canton Viaduct

"Canton Comes of Age 1797–1997," published by Town of Canton, courtesy of Jim Roche, Canton Historical Society. Photo by Mr. Christopher Brindley

The Canton "Viaduct" pictured here was built in 1835. The structure was built by Irish immigrants. The granite was quarried locally in Canton and neighboring Sharon. The Viaduct was the final link between Boston and Providence, Rhode Island. This structure is on the National Historic Register.

"Early View of Freight Traffic across the Viaduct," courtesy of New Haven Railroad Historical & Technical Association Inc., E. D. Galvin Collection. The great stone viaduct at Canton as viewed from above and below. Photo circa 1900

Figure 1-1 (see arrows on illustration) shows the location of where no fewer than ten movable bridges would be required between Williams Bridge and Stonington. Three of these required crossings were wide and deep—at the Housatonic, Connecticut, and Thames rivers. While nine of the ten crossings were bridged using ironwork, the most challenging crossing—the Thames separating New London and Groton, Connecticut—would have to wait for the availability of the steel bridge. James B. Eads first introduced the steel bridge successfully when he crossed the Mississippi River at St. Louis in 1873. The Thames River would not be bridged until 1889 with a steel bridge, at which time most of the earlier iron bridges were also replaced with steel, partly out of concern for safety and partly to accommodate larger and heavier locomotives.

Chapter 3: 1845–1868

Rail All the Way, Plain Vanilla

The twenty-three-year period between 1845 and 1868 was eventful. Beginning as early as December of 1848, it was technically possible to travel by rail all the way between Boston and New York. The little upstart companies of 1845 were maturing to the point that they were regarded as more than just feeders to the steamships on Long Island Sound. The New York and New Haven Railway opened its line between Twenty-Sixth Street and Fourth Avenue, New York City, and New Haven, Connecticut, seventy-four miles east. The first twelve miles from New York to Williams Bridge (later named Woodlawn Junction) would be over the New York and Harlem Railway via leased trackage rights. The remaining sixty-two miles were exclusive New York and New Haven tracks. These sixty-two miles were a building challenge, as five movable bridges had to be installed. This was quite a feat in 1848 (illustration 3-1, see arrows between Williams Bridge and New Haven).

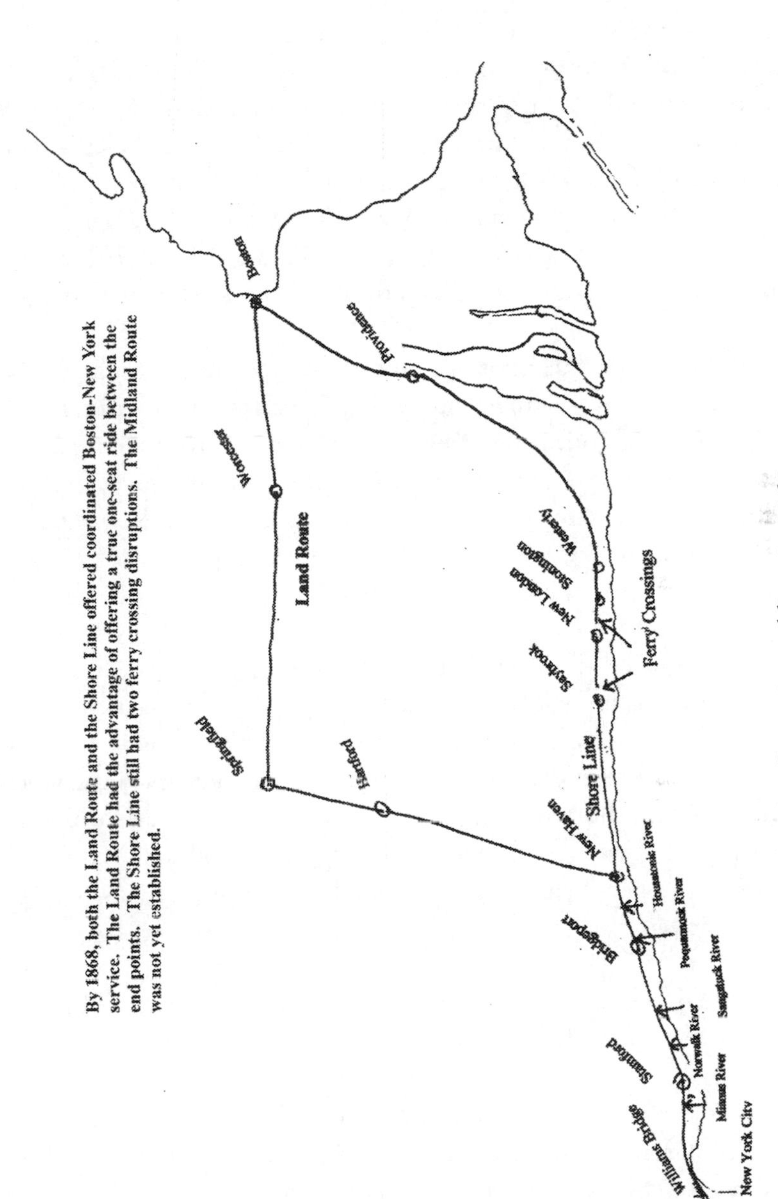
1868 Operating Rail Lines
By 1868, both the Land Route and the Shore Line offered coordinated Boston-New York service. The Land Route had the advantage of offering a true one-seat ride between the end points. The Shore Line still had two ferry crossing disruptions. The Midland Route was not yet established.
Springfield
Worcester
Boston
Land Route
Hartford
Providence
New Haven
Shore Line
Saybrook
New London
Stonington
Westerly
Ferry Crossings
Williams Bridge
Stamford
Bridgeport
Housatonic River
Pequannock River
Norwalk River
Saugatuck River
Mianus River
New York City

3-1 Operating rail lines in 1868

The completion of this link technically opened up an all-land route. In 1849, the traveler left New York City over the tracks of the New York and Harlem Railway. At Williams Bridge, the train veered off onto the tracks of the New York and New Haven Railway. At New Haven, our traveler could change to the cars of the Hartford and New Haven Railway for conveyance through to Springfield. Here the trip could be punctuated for a quick lunch in the station. Then it was on to Worcester over the Western Railroad of Massachusetts with a final change in Worcester to the Boston and Worcester Railway for the trip to Boston. Some fifteen hours and four different seats later, Boston was attained.

The alternative to this rigor and uncertainty would be to use the railway as a feeder to an overnight steamship, perhaps in Providence, and to make the overall journey in about the same time, in greater comfort and with just one change of seats. In 1849, most intercity travelers chose this alternative. Clearly the civil engineering that opened a railway land route was ahead of the technical ability of the railways to provide convenient, rapid, and comfortable travel.

Moving forward from 1849 to 1859, this began to change. Railway technology was improving. The four independent railways that made up the land route began to recognize the value of the through traffic versus just local traffic. Schedules were coordinated, and larger locomotives and better roadbed shortened transit time. A few through cars (no changing seats required) were tried. A solid through-train followed. Gradually the traveling public began to accept the all-land route as something more than an adventure.

By 1859, the Shore Line was completed, save for the lack of bridges over the Connecticut and the Thames rivers (illustration 3-1). The little New Haven and New London Railway, first to call itself the "Shore Line route," opened the fifty-mile route between its namesake cities. Across the Thames River in Groton, Connecticut, the New York, Providence and Boston Railway stretched east sixty-two miles to Providence, Rhode Island. Despite its ambitiously hopeful name, this road never reached New York or Boston via its own rails. But it was a vital link in the evolving Shore Line route. At Providence, through passengers could change to the cars of the Boston and Providence Railway to complete their journey to the Hub City.

The 1868 All-Rail Schedules

Via the "land route," the New York and Boston Express Line

Boston and Albany Railway
New Haven, Hartford and Springfield Railway
New York and New Haven Railway

Leave New York (26th Street)		Arrive Boston	Lv. Boston	Ar. New York
8:00 a.m.	Express	5:05 p.m.	8:30 a.m.	4:55 p.m.
3:00 p.m.	Express	11:50 p.m.	2:30 p.m.	10.50 p.m.
8:00 p.m.	Mail	6:00 a.m.	8:30 p.m.	4:55 a.m.

through fare = $6.00

Via the "Shore Line" route

Boston and Providence Railway
New York, Providence and Boston Railway
New Haven, New London and Stonington Railway
New York and New Haven Railway

Leave New York (26th Street)		Arrive Boston	Lv. Boston	Ar. New York
8:00 a.m.	Accommodation	6:05 p.m.		
12:15 p.m.	Express	9:10 p.m.	11:10a.m.	7:20 p.m.
8:00 p.m.	Mail	6:00 a.m.	8:30 p.m.	5:00 a.m.

From the above schedules, it is clear that the three operators of the New York and Boston Express Line, the land route, were the leaders in getting passengers off the steamships and onto their respective railways. The 1867 merger of the Boston and Worcester with the Western Railway of Massachusetts created the Boston and Albany Railway. The managers of the Boston and Albany together with the connecting New Haven, Hartford and Springfield Railway believed they had the best route. The New York and New Haven Railway was relatively neutral since they were assured of all rail traffic west of New Haven.

The land route would be clearly superior to the Shore Line since it served three major cities between Boston and New Haven, namely Worcester, Springfield, and Hartford. The Shore Line encountered only one major city en route, Providence. Then, too, in 1868 you had a true one-seat ride over the land route, whereas on the Shore Line you still had to encounter the disruptions of the ferry crossings over the Connecticut and Thames rivers. The 160 miles of the land route from Boston to New Haven compared with 157 miles via the Shore Line was considered inconsequential.

As for steamship competition, the land route promoters offered a choice of two day trains as well as one by night. The steamship companies were always an overnight operation. Finally, with end-point timings down to about eight and a half hours versus fourteen hours via boat, train, and steamship, the railway had the time edge. The apparently longer eastbound timings are accounted for by the lack of standard time in 1868. The clocks of Boston were twelve minutes ahead of New York.

The three operators of the Boston–New Haven Shore Line recognized they had better coordinate some through trains if they wished to compete. They came up with three eastbound through trains and strangely only two westbound counterparts. The third westbound through train originated in Providence, not Boston. The Shore Line end-point times came close to matching the land route.

Aboard the Trains of 1868

Despite the promotion of land routes, express lines, and shore lines, railway travel of the time lacked amenities. The flat-roofed wooden cars or even the early clerestory-roofed cars were hot and sooty in the summer. In the winter the traveler was either too hot or too cold, depending on the distance to the woodstove. The night trains had a primitive sleeping car, little more than a car of barracks-style layered bunk beds where you were expected to bring your own bedding. The day coaches were cramped. There were no first-class parlor cars and no dining service. Travelers grabbed their meals en route from a station lunch counter.

The through trains indicated in the above schedules operated without benefit of numbers or names. The word *express* separated the fast trains from the slower *accommodation* trains. The overnight trains were *mail*. Passengers were tolerated. More powerful 4-4-0 engines had been purchased. They could pull greater loads and run faster. But the technology for controlling increased speeds was still lacking. There were no block signals, no Westinghouse air brakes, and little protection from fire following a wreck where the splintered wooden coaches were torched by the stove embers or the kerosene lanterns. The sound steamers still had the comfort and safety edge in 1868, though even the steamers were not immune to fire or explosions.

Still, it was a beginning to all-rail travel. One can speculate on what might have happened had the Boston and Albany Railway subsequently become a part of the New Haven Railroad rather than going to the Vanderbilts (New York Central) in 1894. Would the manifest destiny of the land route have been realized? Would it have become today's high-speed and preeminent route between Boston and New York rather than the Shore Line? Or did the accident of ownership doom the land route to a secondary status?

Chapter 4: 1868–1893

Riding in Style

Our time jump from 1868 to 1893 is just twenty-five years. In 1868 through rail travel between New York and Boston was still in its infancy. A total of four or five trains a day made the journey over two routes. By 1893, no less than twelve weekday departures each way made the journey with a choice of three competing roads. Virtually every hour on the hour from 9:00 a.m. to 5:00 p.m. trains left the terminal cities. In addition, there were two competing overnight trains that were complete with real sleeping cars from Pullman or Wagner.

In 1893 for the next twenty years, the railroads were at their peak. Each of the three railroads figured their competition came mainly from another railroad and, to a lesser extent, the steamships. The automobile and commercial aviation did not exist.

From Boston, the three routes west to New York were the following:

1. The Inland Route via Worcester, Springfield, and Hartford
2. The Willimantic Route (also called the Middle, Midland, and Air Line route) via Putnam, Willimantic, and Middletown
3. The Shore Line Route via Providence and New London (illustration 4-1)

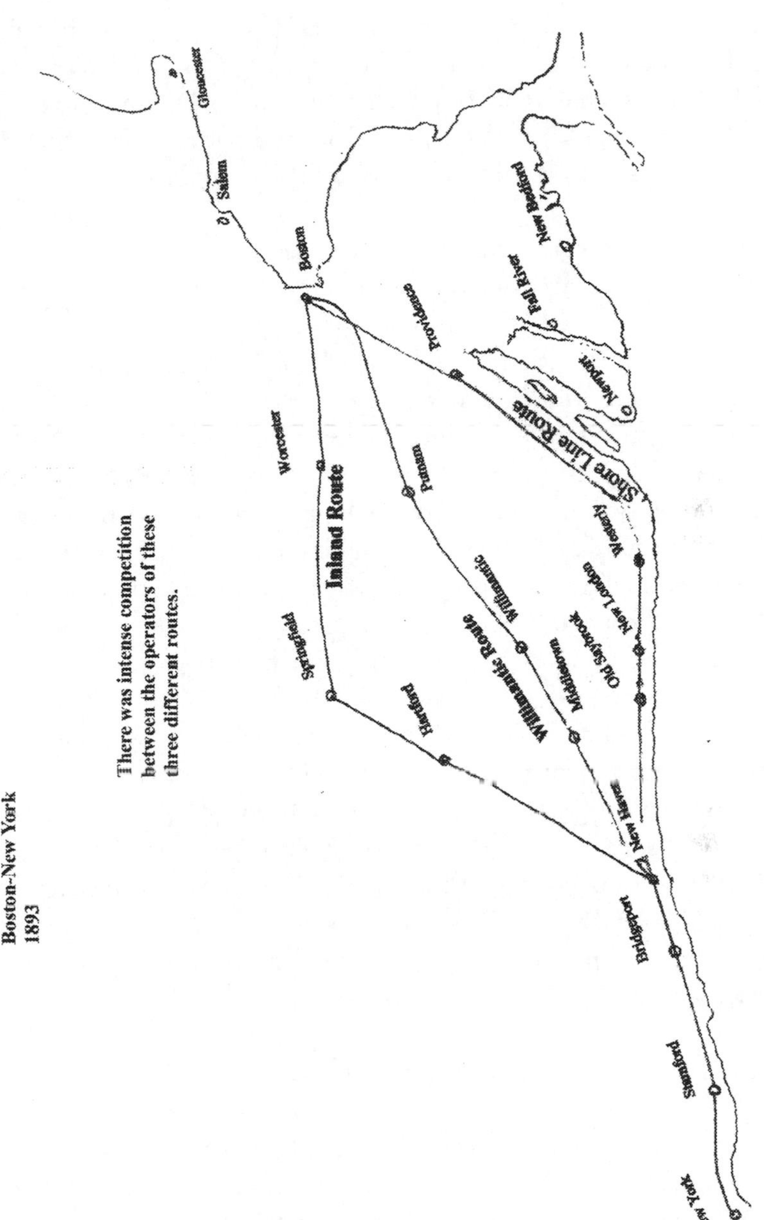

4-1 Three routes between Boston and New York City, 1893

The year 1893 was the height of the wooden passenger-car era. Trains carried day coaches, parlor cars, and dining cars. The parlor cars in particular were elaborately decorated with elegant stained glass windows and inlaid woods. Parlor car seats were overstuffed with Victorian tassels and footrests. The woodstove was gone, and steam heat was in. Gas illuminated the cars instead of kerosene lamps. Open vestibules and flat roofs gave way to vestibuled cars for safety and clerestory roofs for better ventilation.

The roadbed now had ballast for better drainage and steel rails instead of iron. The frail iron bridges gave way to steel crossings.

The 4-4-0 American locomotive still reigned but with larger fireboxes, higher boiler pressure, larger cylinders, and greater tractive effort. Drive wheel diameter grew from sixty-three to seventy-nine inches for speed. On the express trains, trip times shrank from eight and a half hours to five hours and forty minutes. Brakes could now be applied to all cars from the engine by using the new Westinghouse air brake. Prior to this, the engineer had brakes only on the engine. If he needed additional car braking, he would have to whistle his request to the trainmen who would rush to the open vestibules to set the brake on each car one car at a time.

But with the big buildup in speed, more than air brakes were needed for safety. Collisions were all too frequent. There were only scattered applications of block signals to indicate the condition of the track ahead. Manned signal towers were placed ten to fifteen miles apart, and it was here that the tower operator gave the engineer permission to proceed at least as far as the next tower. The wooden cars themselves, while elegant and ornate, still splintered on impact and offered little protection. All-steel cars were needed but slow in coming.

The West End, a Congested Powerhouse

The West End refers to all track west of New Haven to New York City. This seventy-four-mile stretch of track was the main artery of the Boston–New York rail lines. All three routes from Boston fed into it at New Haven. There simply was no way to avoid this line if you were bound from southern New England to New York City. The double-tracked West End became so congested that by 1890 work began on four tracking the entire route (illustration 4-2).

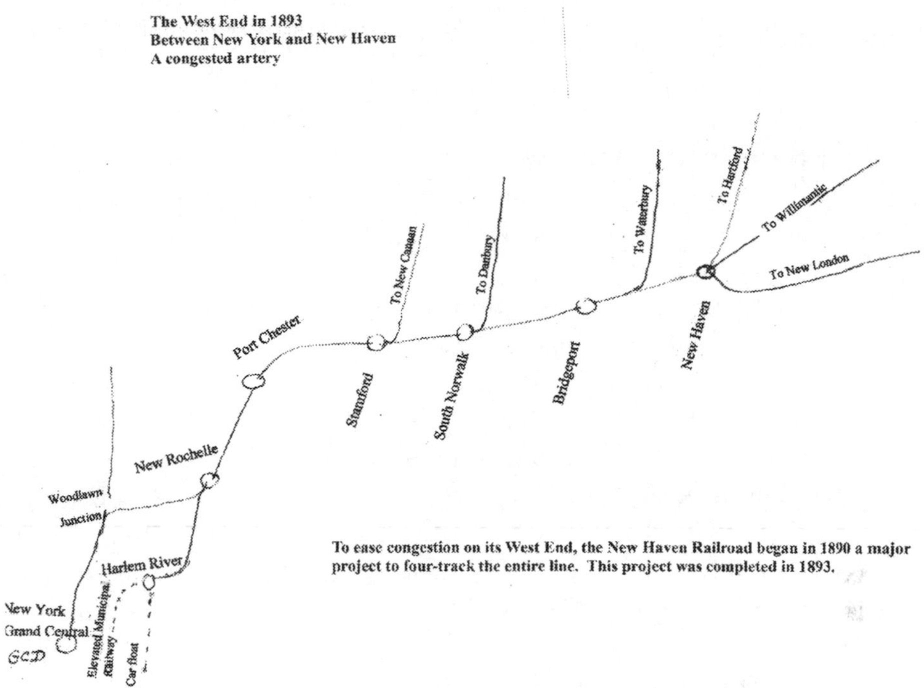

4-2 The West End in 1893 (between New York and New Haven)

Perhaps this traffic density is why the original New York and New Haven Railway became the driving force in consolidating the many short lines that together formed the through Boston–New York routes. This consolidation began in 1872 when the New York and New Haven merged with the Hartford and New Haven to form the New York, New Haven and Hartford Railroad, a name that would survive the next ninety-six years. This company, simply the New Haven as it was later called, would gain a virtual transportation monopoly by buying or leasing rail companies south of the Boston and Albany Railway. The New York, Providence and Boston joined the fold in 1892 (along with the former New Haven, New London and Stonington). The Old Colony lines (along with the Boston and Providence) were leased in 1893. These moves gave the consolidated New Haven Railroad full control of the Shore Line Route between Boston and New York. For good measure, the great consolidator acquired the Old Colony lease of the Fall River Line and its fleet of four steamboats that shuttled between New York and Newport or New York and Fall River.

Not fully in the control of the New Haven were the two other land routes via Springfield and via Willimantic.

The 1893 Rail Schedules

Via the Inland Route or Springfield Line

Boston and Albany Railway	98 miles
New York, New Haven and Hartford Railroad	136 miles
Boston–New York route distance	234 miles

Eastbound			Westbound		
Lv. New York 42nd St. Grand Central Depot		Ar. Boston	Lv. Boston		Ar. New York Grand Central D.
9:00 a.m.	Day Express	3:30 p.m.	9:00 a.m.	Day Express	3:30 p.m.
11:00 a.m.	Special Fast Exp.	5:30 p.m.	11:00 a.m.	Spec. Fast Exp.	5:30 p.m.
Noon	New York Ltd. (Parlor cars only)	5:40 p.m.	Noon	New York Ltd. (Parlor cars only)	5:40 p.m.
4:00 p.m.	Fast Line	10:00 p.m.	4:00 p.m.	Fast Line	10:00 p.m
11:00 p.m.	Night Express	6:41 a.m.	11:00 p.m.	Night Express	6:15 a.m

Since this was no longer the exclusive land or all-rail route as was the case in 1868, the land route became simply the Inland Route, a designation that survives to this day. The Springfield Line was another defining moniker.

The still-independent Boston and Albany Railway wanted this route to succeed. The under-two-and-a-half-hour timing of several Boston–Springfield trains was bold. Those 4-4-0 engines had their work cut out for them, given ninety-eight miles filled with curves and grades. In fairness, the New Haven cooperated, hurrying these five Boston and Albany trains over its 136 miles between Springfield and New York. The six- to six-and-a-half-hour end-point times of three day trains compared precisely with the Shore Line timings. The all-parlor *New York Limited* at five hours and forty minutes set a new record for Boston–New York travel and was matched precisely by the Shore Line's *Flyer*, also all-parlor car. The night trains on both roads ran on a somewhat more leisurely schedule.

This was the era when the well-heeled customer had access to drawing-room cars or parlor cars. These passengers also had access to food service via the drawing-room car buffet. Only the 4:00 p.m. *Fast Express* had a full dining car that was open to coach and parlor-car passengers, and this only between Boston and Springfield. Compared to 1868, the lowly day-coach passenger had a faster ride but not much more comfort or other amenities.

By 1893, a travel pattern was developing. Business travelers from Boston or New York would begin the journey via an overnight train or an overnight steamship, arriving at their destination at the beginning of the business day. After they had spent one or several days engaged in their commercial endeavors, they were ready to journey home by 4:00 or 5:00 p.m. via the train. This would get them back home in their own beds that night rather than spending it en route.

Although there was nothing bold about the rather generic names assigned to the Inland Route trains, they did, for the first time, have names and each train had a number.

These 1893 schedules would prove to be the peak frequency of Inland Route service. Never again would we see an all-parlor train on this route. Never again would we see five trains each way every weekday. This is the last time the New Haven Railroad would settle for parity.

Via the Shore Line

New York, New Haven and Hartford Railroad 231 miles

Eastbound Lv. New York 42nd St. Grand Central Depot		Ar. Boston	Westbound Lv. Boston		Ar. New York 42nd St. Grand Central Depot
10:00 am	Day Express	4:30 pm	10:00 am	Day Express	4:30 pm
1:00 pm	Afternoon Exp.	7:30 pm	1:00 pm	Afternoon Exp.	7:30 pm

2:00 pm	Shore Line Flyer All parlor cars	7:40 pm	2:00 pm	Shore Line Flyer All parlor cars	7:40 pm
5:00 pm	Gilt Edge Limited	11:00 pm	5:00 pm	Gilt Edge Ltd.	11:00 pm
Midnight	Midnight Express	7:00 am	Midnight	Midnight Exp.	7:00 am

The service pattern was strikingly similar to the Inland Route. The day opened with two six-and-a-half-hour trains. Then came the all-parlor *Flyer*, a five-hour-and-forty-minute train, followed by a six-hour trip and closing with the night train. Only the late-afternoon train carried a full dining car and only between Boston and New London. The 5:00 p.m. train, *Gilt Edge Limited*, was a first step in introducing more fanciful or route-specific names. The New Haven Railroad of the time was considered a sound, lucrative, and enduring investment—"widows and orphans" stock whose certificates were said to be gilt-edged. Did a bit of braggadocio creep into the naming of this train?

Via the Willimantic Route (or Air Line)

Via New York and New England Railroad	to Willimantic 86 miles to Hartford 117 miles
New York, New Haven & Hartford	from Willimantic to N.Y. 127 miles from Hartford to N.Y. 110 miles total Boston–New York via Willimantic = 213 miles Via Hartford = 227 miles

Eastbound Lv. New York 42nd St. Grand Central Depot		Ar. Boston	Westbound Lv. Boston		Ar. New York, 42nd St. Grand Central Depot
12:03 pm	*Mid-Day Express*	6:30 pm	12:01 pm	*Mid-Day Exp.*	6:30 pm
3:00 pm	New England Ltd. *White Train*	8:40 pm	3:00 pm	New England Ltd. *White Train*	8:40 pm

"superb equipment of parlor cars, coaches, royal buffet smoker and dining car"

The Willimantic Route via Middletown had one advantage over either the Inland Route or the Shore Line. It was twenty-one miles shorter than the Inland and eighteen miles shorter than the Shore Line. This Air Line was indeed the shortest distance between the end points. Beyond this, the Air Line managed to miss any major population centers between Boston and New Haven. At Willimantic, just eighty-six miles from Boston, the New York and New England surrendered the train to the New Haven for the balance of its trip. The *Mid-Day Express*, which would take a longer route, managed to stay on its own tracks from Boston to Hartford, 117 miles.

The New York and New England Railway came up short on financial stability and was embarrassingly thin on population. Between Boston and New Haven, the population centers were the towns of Franklin, Blackstone, Putnam, Willimantic, and Middletown.

Only two trains each way were scheduled, no match for the five each of their two competitors offered. How to make the best of the situation? Match the competition on timings and beat them with pizzazz.

The *New England Limited* was selected for the marketing blitz. Its cars were all white, quite a stunning contrast to the dark-hued cars of the time. The diner operated through from Boston to New York. The little New York and New England matched the five-hour-and-forty-minute timing of the all-parlor car flyers of the competition. In recognition of their thinly populated route, and their likely inability to fill an all-parlor car train, the *White Train* did accept coach passengers. Only on the *New England Limited* did the Boston–New York coach traveler have access to such speed and luxury. We have no reports on how this egalitarianism played out with the Boston Brahmins.

To make the fast schedule, the *New England Limited* skipped the stops at Franklin, Blackstone, and Putnam, leaving only Willimantic and Middletown to fatten the passenger lists out of Boston.

The second train, *Mid-Day Express*, matched the slower six-and-a-half-hour timings of their competitors' day expresses. The Hartford route at 227 miles, while longer than the Air Line, was still a bit shorter than either the Inland Route or the Shore Line. The *Mid-Day Express* made the stops missed by the *White Train* and also served Hartford, Connectict, providing some competition with the Inland Route. Still, the *Mid-Day Express* lacked any food service. Passengers riding in those elegant parlor cars apparently had to bring their own sandwiches.

Twelve Weekday Trains Each Way in Perfect Symmetry

In viewing the complete rail offering between Boston and New York, each road had an almost slavish adherence to symmetry. If the road had a six-hour train leaving New York at 5:00 p.m., this same road had a precise counterpart leaving Boston at 5:00 p.m. There may have been some collusion amongst the competitors. All day trains left their end point on the hour *every hour* from 9:00 a.m. to 5:00 p.m., making it easy for people who hated to read timetables. Only the noon trains were duplicated on two roads. At all other hourly marks, just one road had a train, and there were no gaps in the 9:00 a.m. to 5:00 p.m. hourly departures.

The Harlem River Branch

The twelve weekday trains that linked Boston and New York in 1893, the subject of this chapter, would not be complete without mention of two additional weekday trains that operated out of Boston but only "sort of" stopped in New York. These two trains, the *Colonial Express* by day and the *Washington Express* by night journeyed down the shoreline for 215 of its 231 miles. When these trains reached New Rochelle, they diverged off the main line and onto the Harlem River branch, proceeding another twelve miles to the end of rail at a Harlem River ferry wharf in the Bronx.

This twelve-mile branch was built in 1872. The reason was the need to establish an all-rail freight connection with New York City and to provide through freight car connections with lines operating west and south of New York City.

Prior to the Civil War (1861–1865) the pattern of railroad freight traffic was similar to the early passenger trains. The little independent railroads linked local industries with local markets. Longer-distance traffic was hauled to ports for transfer to steamships. Few railcars were interchanged between the little roads.

After the Civil War, this began to change. The maturing railroads began to interchange cars, and freight was staying on the rails for the entire trip. In 1872, the New York and New Haven Railway merged with the Hartford and New Haven Railway to form the New York, New Haven and Hartford Railroad (the New Haven). The newly expanded railroad immediately faced two vexing freight problems: (1) where to terminate an all-rail freight movement to New York City and (2) where and how to interchange with connecting roads to the west and south given the barrier of the Hudson River.

On the West End, the New Haven Railroad owned its own tracks only to Woodlawn Junction. By 1870, Cornelius Vanderbilt had acquired ownership of the two railroads that directly served Manhattan Island, namely the Hudson River Railroad, with excellent freight car handling facilities on the west side, and the New York and Harlem Railway with poor freight handling facilities (illustration 4-3). Vanderbilt developed a plan to merge his two New York City properties. He would discontinue the passenger terminal at Twenty-Sixth Street and Fourth Avenue, moving the new terminal almost one mile north to Forty-Second Street and Park Avenue. Here he would build a Grand Central Depot (opened in 1872). He would build a Harlem River connecting railroad between Spuyten Duyvil and Morris Park, linking the two railroads. The Hudson River Railroad would be routed away from its ancestral terminal at Thirtieth Street and Eleventh Avenue (out of the way) to his palatial new Grand Central Depot, much more central to the city and soon to be accessible via the Manhattan Elevated Railway. The connector would benefit the New York and Harlem Railway by giving it access to the freight facilities on the west side. While Vanderbilt had no problem with leasing his tracks for New Haven *passenger* trains from Woodlawn Junction to the new Grand Central Depot, he was not about to share his prized freight facilities. The best solution for the desperate New Haven Railroad was to build a twelve-mile branch from New Rochelle to tidewater at the Harlem River at 133rd Street and to another tidewater site two miles north called Oak Point. At these wharves goods could be transferred to teams of horses and wagons for the six-mile ride down to lower Manhattan, where the consumers and wholesalers lived. The Harlem River branch was an immediate success and was double tracked for the entire distance, including two movable bridges. By 1880 a barge was designed to accept freight cars rolled right aboard on tracks and secured for transport through the protected waters of the East River and the Upper New York harbor. A tugboat, separate from the barge, provided propulsion. The tug and railroad barge pretty well solved both New Haven Railroad problems. Freight cars were floated from the Harlem River wharf to piers and warehouses in lower Manhattan, to Brooklyn, and to Long Island. The car-float system soon extended right across the upper harbor to connect with railroads that ended at the New Jersey shoreline. The Pennsylvania Railroad, the Central Railroad of New Jersey, and the Lehigh Valley Railroad were all eager partners in opening up the west and the south to the New Haven Railroad. The old river barrier became a waterborne rail-connecting highway. Vanderbilt and the New York Central be damned! The New Haven Railroad had wiggled around the problem by 1880.

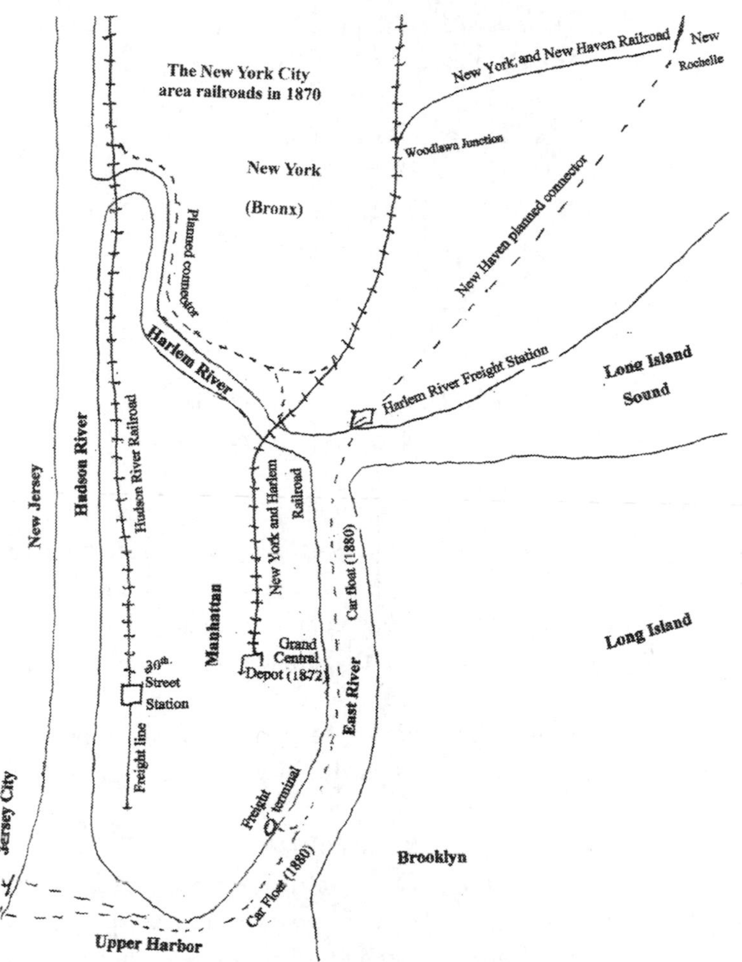

4-3 New York City area railroads in 1870

If freight could go right through from New England to Philadelphia, Baltimore, and Washington, DC, why not a passenger train too? Indeed they could. In the early 1880s, the Pennsylvania Railroad and the New Haven Railroad joined forces by designing and building a double-ended passenger ferry that could accept the entire train of passenger cars right on board (except the engine). The result was the *Steamer Maryland.* This special vessel was able to navigate the twelve miles from Harlem River to Jersey City in about one hour and fifteen minutes. The actual docking in New Jersey was not at Exchange Place, the Pennsylvania's main station. Instead the *Steamer Maryland* used the freight docks at adjoining Harsimus Cove, a short distance north of Exchange Place.

The 1893 schedules of these two boat-trains follows:

Lv. Washington, DC		Ar. Boston	Lv. Boston		Ar. Washington, DC
3:15 pm	Boston Exp. daily	7:30 am	7:30 pm	Washington Exp. daily	10:42 am
7:50 am	Colonial Exp. except Sunday	8:30 pm	9:00 am	Colonial Exp. except Sunday	9:45 pm

The night trains were praised for their vestibuled cars. They carried sleeping cars with buffets between Boston and Philadelphia, Boston and Washington, and even Boston and Jacksonville, Florida. Alas, 1893 was not the time to cater to the day coach passenger. The night trains carried day coaches from Boston to Philadelphia, where presumably the huddled masses had to scramble for a connecting train to continue their southward journey. The day train, the *Colonial Express*, carried vestibuled parlor cars and coaches all the way to Washington, but never on Sundays.

These trains were an instant success, affirming the need for through passenger service from Boston to points south and west of New York City. West and southbound passengers arriving in the 1872 Grand Central Depot were in for a struggle getting over to a continuing train in Jersey City.

The Harlem River branch became a four-track railroad after 1882 as traffic increased. New Haven management viewed the branch as their very own line to New York City. They even toyed with the idea of diverting some Shore Line expresses down the branch to terminate at their 133rd Street passenger terminal, somewhat west of the freight docks. Here a bridge and a connecting shuttle train crossed the Harlem River to 129th Street, the 1882 terminal of the Manhattan (elevated) Railway where frequent "el" trains pulled by little Forney steam engines departed via both a Second Avenue and a Third Avenue route for the eight-and-a-half-mile trip to the southern tip of Manhattan Island. This urge to divert was always strongest immediately after the Vanderbilts gave the New Haven Railroad their latest "per car" lease rates for trackage south of Woodlawn Junction. This urge was tempered by the image of parlor car passengers packing onto the bridge shuttle trains and the one-class elevated cars. The New Haven management felt the "per car" lease was particularly outrageous for their suburban trains that had the effect of keeping suburban fares relatively high. If any diversion should be tried, maybe the suburban traffic was the place to do it? By 1893, the Harlem River branch had twenty-one weekday one-way trains that shuttled between New Rochelle and 129th Street for a direct connection with the "el" trains. The combined railroad and "el" fares were lower than the fare on a through commuter train to Grand Central Depot. The service was modestly successful, appealing to the economy customer, willing to trade some time and convenience for a lower fare.

The two boat-trains are not included in our calculations of Boston–New York frequencies. Although these trains technically stopped in New York at the docks of the Harlem River, there is little evidence to show passengers were encouraged to begin or end their journeys in the docklands.

Chapter 5: 1893–1910

Rail at Its Peak

The seventeen years between 1893 and 1910 were full of challenges for the three railroads operating the Boston–New York corridor. Most of the challenges were of the pleasant kind—keeping up with growth, always easier than coping with decline.

Right out of the gate in 1893 was a challenge all three competitors had to face. This challenge was to survive the 1893 panic, which bit deeply into traffic and revenue. The experiences of each of the three were radically different.

Sudden downturns in the gross domestic output of goods and services were natural parts of the business cycle. To the citizens of the nineteenth century, these industrial cycles were a part of their learning curve as they adjusted to the increasingly industrial society that was replacing the agricultural world. When business expanded too fast or borrowed too heavily and bet on tomorrow being better than today, a downturn took the overly leveraged with it. The word *panic* doubtless refers to the hapless creditors, attempting to get their money back from a sinking firm. The word was too alarmist for 1930 America. Instead the word *depression*, as a depression in the road, was considered so much more soothing. The deep and lengthy downturn of the 1930s banished this term too. Now a downturn is simply a *recession*, and everyone should feel better.

One of the three Boston–New York rail lines, the New York and New England Railroad was overly leveraged. In 1893 it was one of many leased roads of the Reading Railroad System, whose flamboyant president, Archibald A. McLeod, tried to string together a northeast rail empire to rival the Pennsylvania Railroad or the New York Central. His empire stretched from Philadelphia to Buffalo to Boston. He was attempting to corner and control the anthracite coal market. The little New York and New England was just the final link in getting anthracite coal over the Poughkeepsie Bridge and into Connecticut and Massachusetts. As the 1893 panic deepened, traffic and revenues fell. Lease payments fell behind. Soon the whole house of cards collapsed. It would take several years for the New York and New England road to get its road back after the lease defaulted and the bankruptcy court sorted it out. When it did retake control in 1895, the New York and New England Railroad (renamed simply the New England) was unable to continue for long. To avoid collapse and possible closure, the directors agreed to another lease—this time to their close rival, the New Haven Railroad. The New Haven monopoly in southern New England grew stronger. One of the three players in the Boston–New York market was gone.

A second player in this market was the Boston and Albany Railway. The B & A directors of 1893 considered their road as a Commonwealth of Massachusetts carrier first and a New England carrier second. Except at the far west end, the relatively few branch lines never left Massachusetts. From their parochial Boston hub, their universe stretched out to where the west began—somewhere around Albany, New York.

The Vanderbilts (New York Central) had built a Northeast–Midwest rail empire by acquiring or leasing lines that put the Central into Cincinnati, Columbus, Indianapolis, Detroit, Chicago, and St. Louis. But they lacked a line into New England. The Vanderbilts had tried before to acquire or lease a New England carrier connecting at Albany, but to no avail. There were only two possibilities—the Boston and Maine (at Troy) or the Boston and Albany (at Albany). The Boston and Albany was the preferred route since it was a relatively straight shot to Boston via the Commonwealth's second and third largest cities. The Boston and Maine was encumbered with too many branch lines, and the B & M directors were not about to sell just the Fitchburg (Troy) Division, their crown jewel. The fiercely independent directors of the Boston and Albany refused to consider the Vanderbilt offers—until the panic of 1893. The Boston and Albany weathered the panic but it spooked the directors. They began to reason that a favorable lease to the Vanderbilts might not be so bad after all. These lease payments, guaranteed by a solid leasee, would inoculate the B & A shareholders from any future panics and shocks. In return for stability and freedom from worry, they signed their lease with the New York Central in 1894. The Boston and Albany name would continue (just as if nothing changed) but the Boston and Albany became an east-west road as never before with consequent downgrading of their role in the Boston–New York market.

The third and final player in the Boston–New York market was the New Haven Railroad. The 1893 panic came up against a financially strong road. To be sure, the traffic downturn required economies, layoffs, schedule cutbacks, and dividend trimming but no default. As traffic rebounded about 1898, the New Haven directors were emboldened enough to enter into a successful lease bid for the New England Railroad.

As the New Haven Railroad entered the 1900–1910 period, the directors were doubtless concerned about how their southern New England transportation monopoly was going to play out in Washington, DC. President Theodore Roosevelt and his "trust busters" had sent shivers down many a corporate spine, witness their treatment of Standard Oil, E. H. Harriman and his Union Pacific–Southern Pacific merger, or James Hill and the Northern Securities Company (merger of the Great Northern, Northern Pacific, and Burlington Lines). Would the trust busters pounce on the New Haven next? This railroad not only bought up or leased virtually all southern New England rail competitors, but they also controlled some leading steamship lines and electric interurban railroads. The key to not being singled out was to offer full service over every formerly competitive route they controlled rather than shutting some down and forcefully diverting passengers. The 1910 New Haven timetable (illustration 5-1) illustrates this effort. Rather than touting just the Shore Line, the directors went out of their way to keep through trains on all three routes, equipping each of them with food service cars and parlor cars.

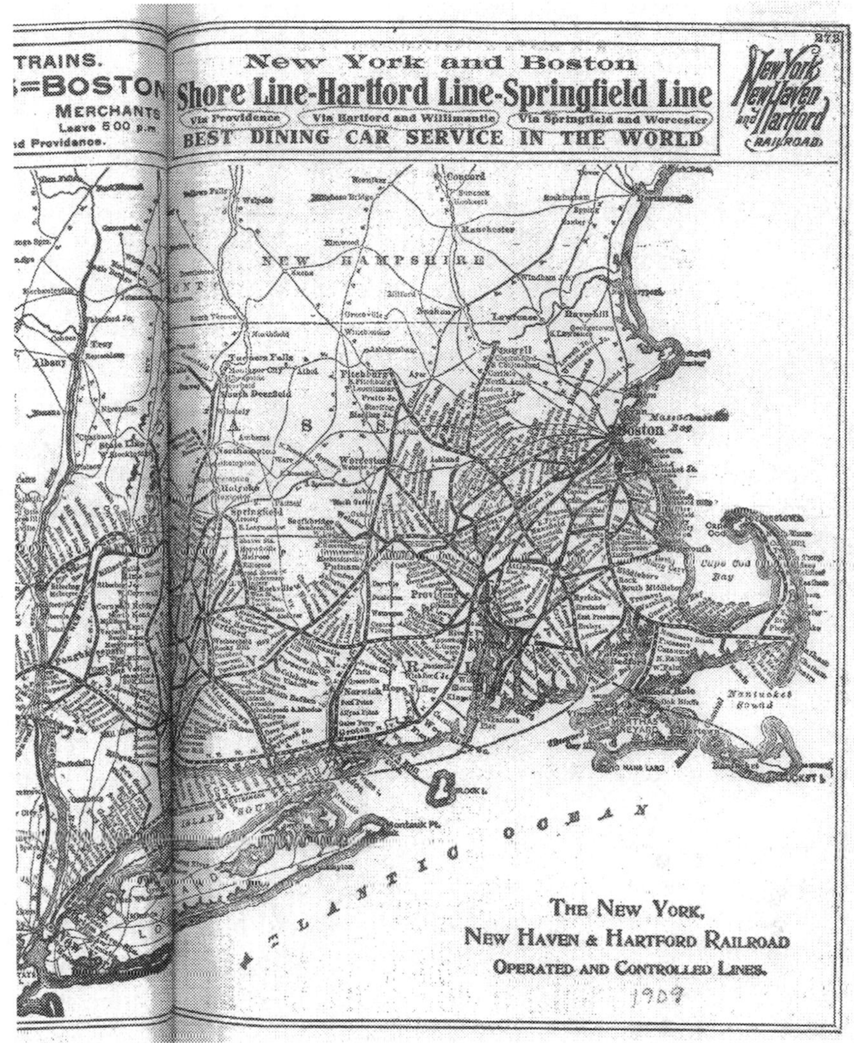

5-1 Boston and New York—three routes in 1893

The directors got through the 1893 panic and the "trust buster" era with only minor injuries and could thus direct their energy to a final and enormous challenge. In 1903 they received a mandate from New York City that stated that by July 1908 no more steam trains could operate into Manhattan Island. Other than an outright withdrawal from Manhattan, the only alternative was to electrify. The New York Central, owner of the tracks from Woodlawn Junction to New York City, had already decided on a 650-volt direct current third rail system, with incoming steam engines changed to electrics at Croton-Harmon and North White Plains. It was assumed that the New Haven would follow suit, establishing a locomotive change point somewhere east of Woodlawn Junction.

The directors concluded otherwise. They reasoned they had a dual-purpose railroad—heavy freight to the Harlem River and passengers to Grand Central. The New York Central low-voltage third rail operation was mainly for passengers. The New York Central Railroad's heavy freight came down the West Shore Line across the Hudson River in New Jersey. Low-voltage direct current just would not cut it for heavy freight—too much voltage drop between sub stations and the rail. Not enough heft for heavy freight trains. Instead, the directors went with eleven-thousand-volt alternating current. The railroad and its suppliers would design engines hauling Grand Central-bound passenger trains with dual power. These engines could operate by drawing power from 650-volt third rail or eleven-thousand-volt power supplied from overhead catenary (wire). Furthermore, this power conversion would be accomplished "on the fly." There would be no need to stop. The New Haven directors reasoned that if they were being forced to electrify some mileage to get into Grand Central, they might as well do it right. After several years of study, a decision was made in 1905 to go with overhead catenary at eleven-thousand-volt AC and to electrify far more than just the entrance strip to Woodlawn Junction. They would put the entire West End (New Haven and west) under wire, including the Harlem River branch. Under the gun to meet the 1908 deadline, electrification work began at Woodlawn Junction and worked east. Work crews had the wire strung east to Stamford, Connecticut, by the deadline, and it was here that engines were changed from steam to straight electric box-cabs. By 1914, the wire was completed all the way east to New Haven. Traffic on the busy four-track West End was in good hands behind clean, efficient electric power. The inevitable next panic of 1913 did not deter the completion of the project. What it did do was put on hold any plans to electrify farther east from New Haven to Boston, at least until the business environment improved. In 1914, few would have believed it would take eighty-seven years (until the year 2000) for this temporary delay to run its course.

The 1910 Boston–New York Weekday Schedules

Via the Inland Route or Springfield Line

Lv. New York		Ar. Boston	Lv. Boston	Ar. New York
9:15 am	New York Day Expr.	3:15 pm	9:15 am	3:15 pm
12:00 noon	Midday Express	5:30 pm	12:00 noon	5:36 pm
4:00 pm	Twilight Express	9:30 pm	4:00 pm	9:35 pm
11:00 pm	Night Express (carries observ. car)	6:25 am	11:30 pm (carries observ. car)	6:25 am

Via the Midland Route Boston–Willimantic–Hartford–New York

Lv. New York		Ar. Boston	Lv. Boston	Ar. New York
8:00 am	Morning Express	1:45 pm	8:00 am	1:45 pm
2:00 pm	Hartford Line Exp.	8:00 pm	2:00 pm	8:00 pm

Via the Shore Line Boston—Providence—New London—New York

Lv. New York		Ar. Boston	Lv. Boston		Ar. New York
10:00 am	Bay State Ltd. (all parlor car)	3:00 pm	10:00 am	Bay State (all parlor car)	3:00 pm
10:02 am	Day Express	4:00 pm	10:02 am	Day Expr.	4:00 pm
1:00 pm	Knickerbocker Ltd. (all parlor car)	6.00 pm	1:00 pm	Knickerbocker Ltd. (all parlor car)	6:00 pm
1:02 pm	Afternoon Express	7:00 pm	1:02 pm	Afternoon Express	7:00 pm
3:00 pm	Shore Line Express	8:30 pm	3:00 pm	Shore Line Express	8:30 pm
5:00 pm	Merchants Ltd. (all parlor car)	10:00 pm	5:00 pm	Merchants Ltd. (all parlor car)	10:00 pm
5:02 pm	Gilt Edge Express	11:00 pm	5:02 pm	Gilt Edge Express	11:00 pm
12:00 mid.	Midnight Express	6:57 am	12:00 mid	Midnight Express	6:57 am

The schedule changes since 1893 were subtle. The New Haven wanted to project its "full service" image over all three routes. Yet the changes were substantial. The Inland Route lost its parity with the ascendant Shore Line. Dropped was the Inland Route's all-parlor train, never to return. Gone were the end point timings equal to the Shore Line. Now the Shore Line enjoyed a clear thirty-minute time advantage. The Inland Route did see a ten-minute reduction in end point times versus 1893, but all of it was due to the Boston and Albany Railroad. The New Haven simply left their Springfield–New York timings intact, refusing to participate in any speedup. The Inland Route's four trains retained their bland names quite in contrast to the sparkle of Shore Line limiteds called *Bay State Limited*, *Knickerbocker Limited*, *Merchants Limited*, or *Gilt Edge Express*.

The former New York and New England didn't fare much better. While the Midland Route retained its two trains, now fully equipped with parlor cars and dining cars, the old sparkle was gone. The *White Train* was removed, replaced first by a less flamboyant *Air Line Express* and finally by an even more nondescript *Morning Express*. The train was moved off of the Willimantic–Middletown–New Haven line in favor of the longer but more populous Willimantic–Hartford–New Haven line. Trip time was increased by five minutes.

By contrast, the Shore Line saw its five 1893 frequencies boosted to eight trains each way. The panache and exclusiveness of riding an all-parlor car extra fare train could be experienced only on the Shore Line. The *Bay State Limited* carried the speed banner in the morning, followed by the *Knickerbocker Limited* in early afternoon and the *Merchants Limited* in late afternoon. These blue-ribbon flyers set a new end-point time record of just five hours, averaging forty-six miles per hour. With five or six wooden cars and a 4-4-2 Atlantic-type engine with seventy-nine-inch drivers, these blistering speeds would not be topped for another twenty-five years.

The Shore Line's remaining trains were longer nine and ten car affairs, dragged by 4-6-2 Light Pacific engines. Their five-and-one-half- to six-hour schedules were unremarkable but fully competitive with the Inland Route. Except for the *Gilt Edge Express*, even their names remained bland and generic, much like the trains on the Inland Route.

In 1910, all trains, regardless of route, changed engines at Stamford, Connecticut, the temporary eastern end of electrification. Trusty box-cab electrics were on the head end for the thirty miles separating Stamford and Grand Central Depot. Year by year, ever-so-gently the New Haven Railroad was positioning the Shore Line as the dominant route. Why share Boston–New York revenues with the Boston and Albany Railroad when you could have it all the way on the Shore Line?

Market Share in 1910

The railway was the clear leader in market share between Boston and New York. The directors of the New Haven Railroad felt pretty secure. After all, they controlled completely two of the three routes and had successfully, if gently, downgraded the third route that they partially controlled. The New England Navigation Company was the New Haven Railroad's umbrella company for most of the formerly independent Long Island Sound steamers. Even in local travel throughout southern New England, the New Haven reigned supreme. Their branch line trains were thriving, and the rival electric trolley companies had been purchased. The personal automobile was still quite a rarity—a rich man's toy. Only the most adventuresome would attempt a Boston–New York trip by automobile and even less so by airplane.

Some Questionable Decisions

In 1910, the New Haven Railroad's board of directors was at the peak of its power and glory. This enormous success may have blinded their judgment on several matters that would eventually lead to serious trouble. Enamored by the speed of their five-hour flyers, the directors held on to lighter wooden coaches all too long. Derailments became disastrous. The directors had been given a second mandate by the New York Central, owner of the soon-to-open Grand Central Terminal. By 1913, wooden passenger cars would no longer be welcome in the New York terminal area. Yet steel cars were not placed widely into service until 1912, and these were reserved for trains that originated or terminated in New York City. Incredibly, the directors placed a substantial order for more wooden coaches for delivery in 1912—for use on non-West end trains.

The other misstep could possibly be called an infatuation—the love of any electric railway. This infatuation was derived from the New Haven's incredible success and recognition that came from its risky, pioneering, and highly successful West End electrification program. The directors came to substitute electric planning for sound planning. In 1906, the New Haven Railroad poured money into start-up trolley companies. Worse, it guaranteed the financing of the New York, Westchester, and Boston Railway, a twenty-one-mile heavy-duty suburban railway that was built from nowhere to nowhere. The line started at the Harlem River (133rd Street) and ended up in White Plains, New York, with a branch line to New Rochelle. Part of the intervening territory was already served by transit lines, and the remaining part ran in sparsely settled suburbia. The design and construction of this line was an electrical engineer's dream. There was a heavy-duty, four-track roadbed, overhead eleven-thousand-volt catenary, high-level loading platforms, and fast-accelerating multiple-unit electric cars. This infrastructure would be the envy of a commuter railroad of 2006. "Build a super electric railroad, and they will come," reasoned the directors. But what if they didn't come, as far too few did?

While hindsight is always with twenty-twenty vision, one still wishes the 1910 directors were a bit more focused on their mainline railroad and less distracted by electrical side shows.

Chapter 6: 1910–1916

Congestion and Troubles

The six years between 1910 and 1916 should have been a period of great growth, efficiency, and profits for the Boston–New York rail carriers. The New Haven Railroad, in particular, would see the completion of its West End electrification program. Overhead power reached down the Harlem River Branch in 1912, to New Haven station in 1914, and right into the Cedar Hill freight yard (New Haven) in 1915. Virtually everything that moved on the West End was entrusted to the efficient electric engines or multiple-unit electric cars. The West End was an efficiency model for the entire country. Traffic kept growing all over southern New England, so much so that congestion began to occur. World War I was still "over there" but the buildup to our entry into World War I was underway. Given the ensuing congestion and troubles, profits were elusive.

With the enormous capital outlay of West End electrification barely digested, the New Haven directors had no rest before still more capital demands were on the table. The gigantic Hell Gate Bridge, a joint venture with the Pennsylvania Railroad, was under construction. A new fourteen-mile freight line through Queens and Brooklyn was under construction (to Bay Ridge, Brooklyn). Fifty new "heavy" Pacific engines (4-6-2) with big seventy-nine-inch drivers were soon to be delivered. When would the enormous capital demands subside and let some profits slide down to the bottom line and out to the investors? In addition to the capital outlays, there were the legendary New Haven Railroad derailments that often became disasters during the 1911–1913 wooden car era. Pressure was on the railroad to put more steel cars on the road, a pressure that was mandated in 1913 for trains entering New York City's brand-new Grand Central Terminal.

The outlays for electrification had depleted the treasury just as the big traffic increase exposed the railroad's lack of hefty motive power, particularly on the Maybrook freight line. Even the Boston–New Haven passenger engines, the biggest of which were light or medium Pacifics (illustration 6-1), were straining to carry ever-heavier all-steel trains. The heavy Pacifics of 1916 arrived none too soon. The 4-6-0 ten-wheelers and 4-4-2 "Atlantics" were already too light and therefore obsolete.

6-1 A Trim Boston and Maine Pacific-type steam engine
Author's collection

Worcester, the second largest city in Massachusetts, featured a Union Station where the Inland Route trains for the Boston and Albany Railroad stood side by side the trains of the New Haven Railroad and the Boston and Maine Railroad. The joint New Haven–Boston and Maine roundhouse stabled a fleet of trim Pacifics, one of which is seen here (Boston and Maine #5529). As late as the early 1950s they headed up B & M trains for Peterboro, New Hampshire, Boston via Ayer, and the Fitchburg line as well as via Sterling Junction and the Central Massachusetts line. They also headed up a New Haven line round trip from Worcester to Providence.

The 1916 Boston–New York passenger schedules would reflect the above realities. Frequencies would increase (illustration 6-2), but average end-point speeds would fall (illustration 6-3), the first speed reversion since the beginning of service.

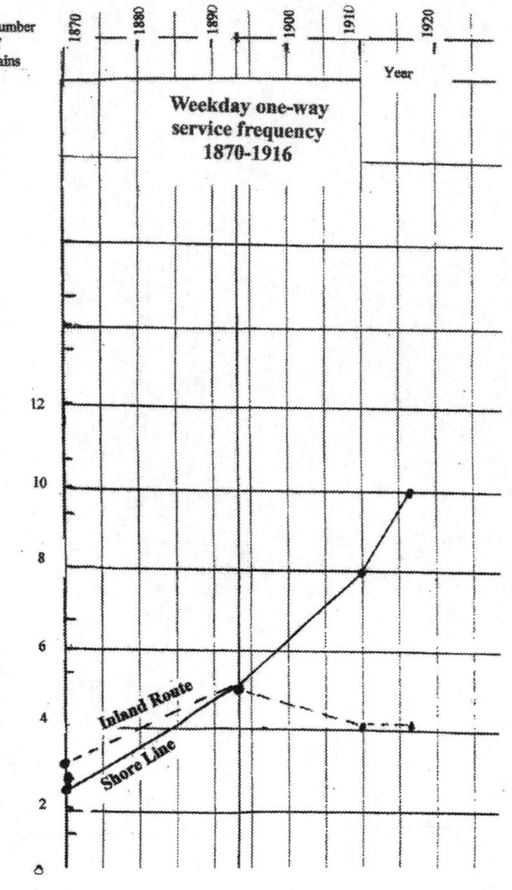

The Inland Route was the frequency leader in 1870. The Shore Line drew up to an equal position in 1893. Once ***the great consolidator*** established its control, the Inland Route never had a chance.

6-2 Weekday service frequency, 1870 to 1916

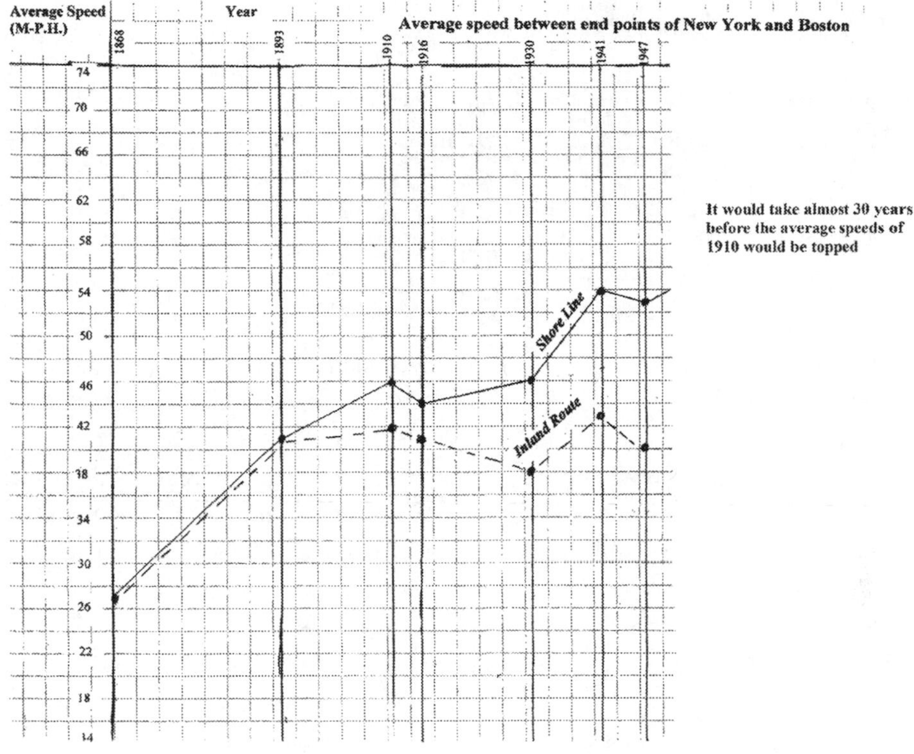

6-3 Weekday speed from 1868 to 1947

The 1916 Boston–New York Weekday Schedules

Via the Inland Route or Springfield Line

Eastbound			Westbound		
Lv. New York		Ar. Boston	Lv. Boston		Ar. New York
9:15 am	Boston Express	3:30 pm	9:15 am	Boston Exp.	3:28 pm
12 Noon	Boston Express	5:55 pm	12 Noon	Boston Exp.	6:06 pm
4:00 pm	Boston Express	9:55 pm	4:00 pm	Boston Exp.	10:04 pm
11:15 pm	Boston Express	6:30 am	11:40 pm	Boston Exp.	7:05 am

Via Willimantic–Hartford–Waterbury

Eastbound		Westbound	
7:51 am	2:30 pm	7:55 am	2:37 pm
2:00 pm	8:31 pm	2:00 pm	8:32 pm

Via the Shore Line

Eastbound			Westbound		
8:30 am	Shore Line Express	2.21 pm	8:30 am	Shore Line	2:19 pm
10:00am	Bay State Ltd. parlor cars only	3:10 pm	10:00 am	Bay State Ltd. parlor cars only	3:10 pm
10:03 am	Shore Line Express	4:10 pm	10:05 am	Shore Line	4:11 pm
1:00 pm	Knickerbocker Ltd. parlor cars only	6:10 pm	1:00 pm	Knickerbocker parlor cars only	6:10 pm
1:03 pm	Shore Line Express	7:00 pm	1:05 pm	Shore Line	7:11 pm
3:00 pm	Shore Line Express	8:43 pm	3:00	pm Shore Line	8:45 pm
5:00 pm	Merchants Limited parlor cars only	10:10 pm	5:00 pm	Merchants parlor cars only	10:10 pm
5:10 pm	Shore Line Express	11:03 pm	5:34 pm	Shore Line	11:15 pm
12 nite	Midnight Express	6:55 am	12:00 nite	Midnight Exp.	6:53 am
12:30 am	The Owl sleeping cars only nonstop	7:05 am	12:30 am	The Owl sleeping cars only nonstop	6:57 a.m

The 1916 schedules were a regression from 1910 in a number of ways.

The Inland Route trains saw their end-point average speeds drop below forty miles per hour. Most trains were given twenty-five to thirty minutes added time to make their journeys. There were still four daily departures, three by day and one by night. The day trains continued to carry food service cars and parlor cars. A new feature of the night train was a set-out sleeper at Worcester. In 1910, the New Haven Railroad had a successful Providence–New York set-out sleeper. The Boston and Albany enjoyed similar success with their Worcester car. Sleeping car passengers could occupy their space as early as 9:30 or 10:00 p.m. and could retain occupancy of their space on the early-arriving set-out cars until 7:30 a.m. Gone from the Inland route were earlier fledging efforts to give a little shine to the trains by giving them more than a generic name. In 1916, they all reverted to being simply Boston Expresses via Springfield. The New Haven Railroad did the same for all Shore Line trains except the three all-parlor-car flyers. Every other day train became simply a Shore Line Express. More running time was added to the Shore Line trains, and even the three flyers were not spared, suffering an added ten minutes in their trip times.

The poor old Midland Route did even worse—no names at all. By 1916, the two through trains on the Midland Route were on their last legs. Yes, you could still get on in Boston or New York and travel through to the other terminal. But trip times were lengthened to as much as six and a half hours. No food service or parlor car service was available. The two surviving trains traveled from Boston to Willimantic, thence to Hartford and Waterbury before rejoining the main line at Bridgeport, Connecticut. It is unclear just how many through passengers would use these two trains. The Midland Route would cease to be a through route by our next look-in year of 1930.

The New Haven Railroad did add two trains to the Shore Line after 1910. One was an 8:30 a.m. generic shoreline express that was meant largely to replace the 1910 Midland Route's morning express. The other train was a result of the growing popularity of the night train. With coaches, head-end cars, through sleepers, and the Providence set-out car, the night train had grown from eight or nine wooden cars to a consist of fourteen to sixteen steel cars. Even on their leisurely night schedules, the consist was straining the capacity of the earlier Pacific (4-6-2) engines. Always averse to double heading (two engines working in tandem), the night train was frequently operated in two sections. The management reasoned that they might as well get some promotion out of this. The second section of the *Midnight Express* would become the all-sleeping-car and nonstop *Owl.* It would be up to the first section to carry the head-end cars, the coaches, make the local stops, and handle the Providence set-out sleeper.

Gone completely was any effort to promote all three Boston–New York routes. The availability of an Inland Route and a Midland Route was buried deep in the timetable. The Shore Line, featured up front in the timetable, was presumably the only sensible through route as far as the New Haven Railroad management was concerned. Were it not for Framingham and Worcester, both good traffic generators, the New Haven might have tried to bury the Inland Route altogether. Springfield and Hartford passengers could be linked to New York via other trains.

Two more casualties of the 1916 retrenchment were the Boston–Washington boat trains via the *Steamer Maryland*. The removal of these two trains on the eve of the opening (1917) of the Hell Gate Bridge with its promise of an expanded Boston–Philadelphia–Washington, DC, service is amazing. The two boat trains were popular. To kill the through trains only to start them up again in another year is probably a testament to just how congested the freight docks and car barges were. After 1916, the situation would only get worse as the United States neared its entry into the war. In fact, in 1917, the railroads throughout the country were in near-gridlock and collapse. The US government, relying heavily on the rail carriers, had no choice but to take over the operation of all railroads in the country, if for no other reason than to keep the war effort going. The United States Railroad Administration (USRA) was formed and ran the national rail system from 1918 to 1920 when the lines were returned to their owners. The railroads learned a painful lesson that they would not repeat in World War II. Equipment and plant must be kept up to date to handle such surges in business. Better care was needed in determining how capital would be spent.

Market Share in 1916

In 1916, the Boston–New York rail lines still had the overwhelming share of the through business. The steamship lines retained their smaller overnight niche. The automobile was growing in importance but was still a minor player in overall market share. The sad truth is that 1916 would be our last look-in year when rail was still the dominant leader in market share. Instead of taking advantage of this supremacy and adding more and faster trains, the rail carriers had all they could handle with their regressive 1916 schedules. They were unable to meet the need for more public transportation when it was needed most. The public, once burned by this poor service, would not soon forget. Other options, notably the private automobile, were looking better.

Chapter 7: 1916–1929

World War I and the Roaring Twenties

The thirteen years between 1916 and 1929 began with frustrating congestion and near paralysis. Between 1918 and 1920, the US government (US Railroad Administration) took over and ran the nation's railroads, sorting out the congestion and opening the way to move war materials and troops. No new capital programs could get underway, just the essentials. By 1920, the private railroads finally had their operations back in hand.

From 1920 and on through the 1920s, prosperity was at hand once again. The Boston–New York rail carriers were conservative, considering the fact that one of their biggest capital investments opened. The Hell Gate Bridge gave the Boston–New York travelers a new route option. They could ride through from Boston to New York's brand-new Grand Central Terminal, or they could ride over the Hell Gate Bridge and enter an equally new and splendid Pennsylvania Station. While the additional Penn Station trains did not terminate there, they did give travelers a big increase in frequency (illustration 7-1). The big frequency buildup kept through patronage at a high level. The New Haven and the Boston and Albany Railroads were also doing well with their suburban commuter operations out of New York and Boston. This passenger growth masked somewhat the big decline occurring on local trains elsewhere on the two systems. The family in New Britain, Connecticut, was no longer piling onto the local train for a day of shopping and fun nine miles away in the big city of Hartford. Instead, they were jumping into the family automobile. This was bad news for the New Haven Railroad, especially as heavily invested as it was in branch lines and electric trolley companies. Branch line passenger schedules were pruned. Older locomotives and cars once found a second home here after serving their prime years on the mainline. Now they had nowhere to go but the scrap heap.

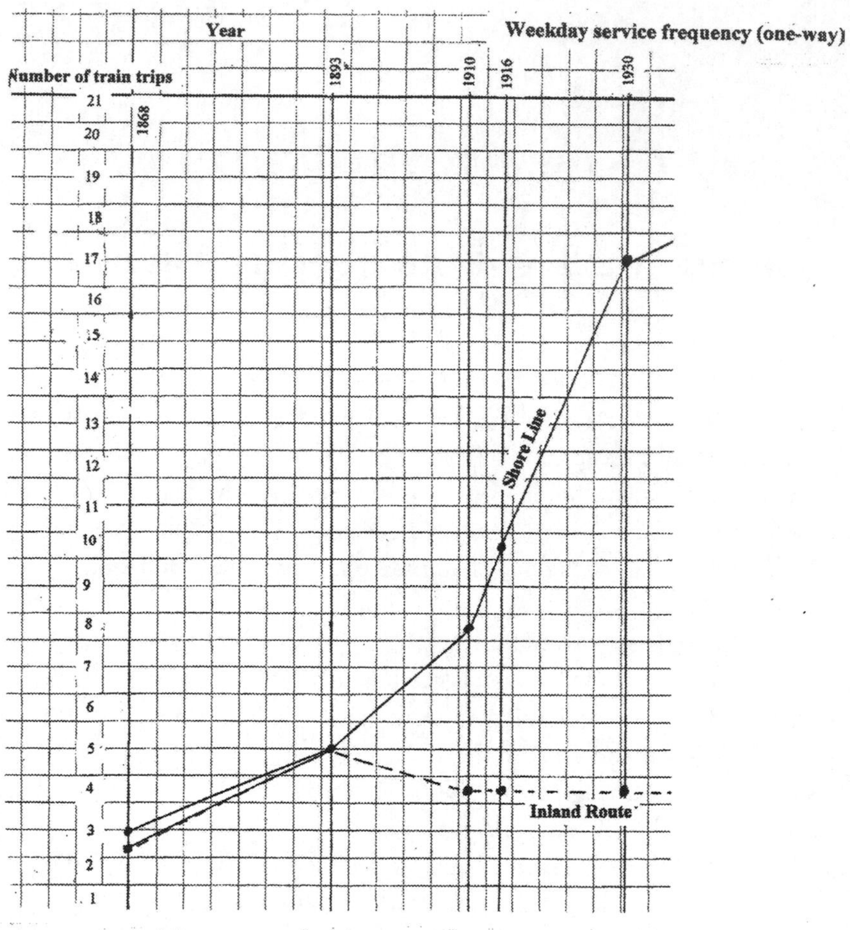

Service frequency exploded between 1916 and 1930 largely due to the opening of Hell Gate Bridge Route. No solid Inland Route trains were given access to the Bridge. Only Shore Line Route trains were given this advantage.

7-1 Weekday service frequency, 1868 to 1930

The year 1917 was to be a grand and glorious year when the massive and remarkable Hell Gate Bridge opened (illustration 7-2). This was the culmination of a grand plan to punch through the water barriers around Manhattan Island that kept the Pennsylvania Railroad and the New Haven Railroad disconnected except for those cumbersome and expensive barge transfers of freight and passengers.

7-2 Hell Gate Bridge circa 1917
Author Detroit Publishing Co.

An article published in 1907 related to the Hell Gate Bridge is quoted at follows:

The Largest Arch Bridge in the World
Scientific American-June 8, 1907

An important feature in the costly improvements being carried out by the Pennsylvania Railroad in and around New York is the building of a connecting railway for uniting the systems of the Pennsylvania Railroad and the New York, New Haven and Hartford Road. This connection will be made by means of a crossing of the East River, the most important feature of which will be an arch bridge (the largest in the world) spanning about a thousand feet. The plans for this bridge have been recently submitted to the Municipal

> Art Commission for its approval in accordance with the franchise granted by this city to the company. The great steel arch will form part of a steel viaduct, itself the largest of its type in the world, the whole length of the structure from abutment on Long Island to abutment in the Bronx being seventeen thousand feet, considerably more than three miles. With a wide, sweeping curve the viaduct will pass over Hell Gate, Ward's Island, Little Hell Gate, Randall's Island, and Bronx Kills. It will be not only the longest but considerably the heaviest steel bridge in existence, with more than eighty thousand tons of steel being needed for its construction. With its completion, the city of New York will find itself in possession of an all-rail route between New England and the South and West. Through trains from Boston may then run to New York, Philadelphia, Baltimore, Washington, Palm Beach, New Orleans, Chicago, St. Louis, or any other southern or western city without leaving the rails. Hitherto cars for such through trains have been ferried around Manhattan Island from the Bronx to Jersey City.

The Problems and the Solution to the Water Barriers

Illustration 7-4 shows the problems of 1905. For the New Haven Railroad, the problem was greatly annoying. For the Pennsylvania Railroad, the problem was growing to catastrophic proportions. The lack of a direct rail connection through New York City was impeding the movement and growth of both freight and passenger traffic.

Freight Traffic

Freight cars moving from southern New England to such southwest points as Philadelphia, Washington, DC, Virginia, the Carolinas, and further south and west temporarily ended their rail journey at the New Haven Railroad's Harlem River or Oak Point yards in the Bronx. Here cars were loaded onto barges for the ten to fourteen-mile trip down the East River and across the upper New York harbor to New Jersey. The New Haven Railroad's cars were towed off the barges at the docks in New Jersey. It didn't matter to the New Haven which docks and which railroads in New Jersey. It could be the Pennsylvania Railroad at Harsimus Cove or Greenville. It could just as well be the docks of the Central Railroad of New Jersey with its connections via the Reading and the Baltimore and Ohio to the same southwest points or even the Lehigh Valley Railroad in Jersey City. The barge operation was an expensive annoyance to the New Haven.

The mighty Pennsylvania Railroad had little leverage over the New Haven. What the Pennsylvania Railroad directors wanted most was a loyal New England partner with whom they could easily exchange eastward traffic and from whom they wished preference on westbound traffic. The New York Central System was the big competitor for the Pennsylvania Railroad. The Central's 1894 lease of the Boston and Albany Railroad enabled the Central to pull a major amount of New England freight traffic for the Midwest through their Albany gateway. This was one carrier service all the way from, say, Boston to Chicago or St. Louis. The Pennsylvania Railroad served virtually all of the same Midwest cities, but it was getting a minor amount of the New England freight traffic. This was an intolerable situation. The solution would be to make the New Haven Railroad a loyal freight-marketing partner and to eliminate the time-consuming and expensive water gap around Manhattan. A new line would be constructed (illustration 7-3), starting at Oak Point. This line would cross the East River at the confluence of Long Island Sound and the Harlem River. A massive four-track bridge, likely to cost 25 to 30 million (in 1905) dollars would do the job. Once over the East River, the new line would roll another fourteen miles through Queens and Brooklyn to a proposed tunnel from Bay Ridge, Brooklyn to Greenville, New Jersey. The portal-to-portal length of this crossing under New York harbor would be four miles. New engineering developments in underwater tunneling and electrically-powered locomotives made this feasible. Such a connection would give the Pennsylvania Railroad an enormous advantage over other New Jersey railroads trying to get to New England. It would make the route competitive with the New York Central for the New England–Midwest service. It would tie the New Haven Railroad closely to its marketing partner, the Pennsylvania Railroad. An interchange track at Fresh Pond Junction (Queens) would feed rail freight traffic to the Long Island Railroad, then an affiliate of the Pennsylvania.

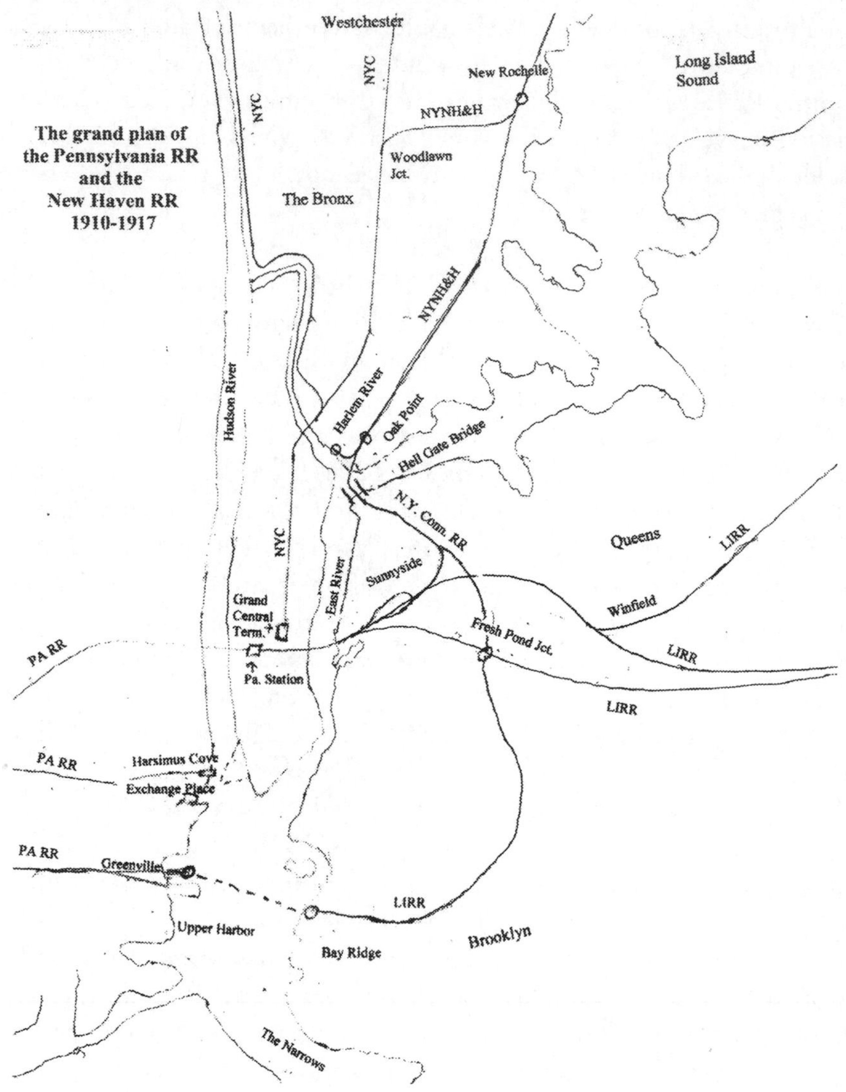

7-3 The grand plan for 1910 to 1917

The New Haven and the Pennsylvania directors agreed to make the Oak Point-Fresh Pond Junction link a joint venture, sharing costs and calling this seven-mile line the New York Connecting Railroad. The Fresh Pond Junction to Bay Ridge link would be the sole construction responsibility of the Pennsylvania Railroad. Its affiliated Long Island Railroad would own the tracks. And what of the four-mile tunnel between Bay Ridge and Greenville? Would the Pennsylvania Railroad go this one alone?

The New Haven directors didn't want any joint venture here. After they had laid out their share of the proposed expenses of the New York Connecting Railroad, including the Hell Gate Bridge, they felt their cupboard would be bare enough. Both parties agreed to let this rest for a while. A marine barge terminal would be established temporarily in Bay Ridge for the three-mile cross-harbor voyage to Greenville, New Jersey. For both parties, this would reduce transit time (versus the Harlem River to Greenville) and allow them to obtain a more efficient use of a smaller marine fleet. This rest would give the New Haven Railroad time to study and observe the results of those new electric freight locomotives planned for the haul from Cedar Hill (New Haven) to the Harlem River. The Bay Ridge line would bring the New Haven into a closer relationship with the Pennsylvania but not as close as the directors of the Pennsylvania Railroad might have liked.

Passenger Traffic

The mighty Pennsylvania Railroad was under the gun in the New York area in 1905. The cumbersome freight transfer by barge gave its competitor, the equally mighty New York Central System a New England–Midwest freight advantage. But this loss in revenue was eclipsed by a looming loss of prestige with passengers. The New York Central had the only railroad station in Manhattan. The big ornate Grand Central Depot of 1872 may have been sooty from steam engines that approached its drafty train shed, but at least the depot was right in midtown Manhattan. It was directly served by an elevated railway plus the just opened (1904) New York subway. By contrast, the Pennsylvania Railroad still occupied its 1871 Exchange Place Station in Jersey City whose ancestral roots traced back to 1834. Exchange Place Station was big, rambling, drafty, and sooty. To get to it, New York City passengers had to make their way to a railroad ferry at the Hudson River and Twenty-Third Street or at Cortland Street (illustration 7-4).

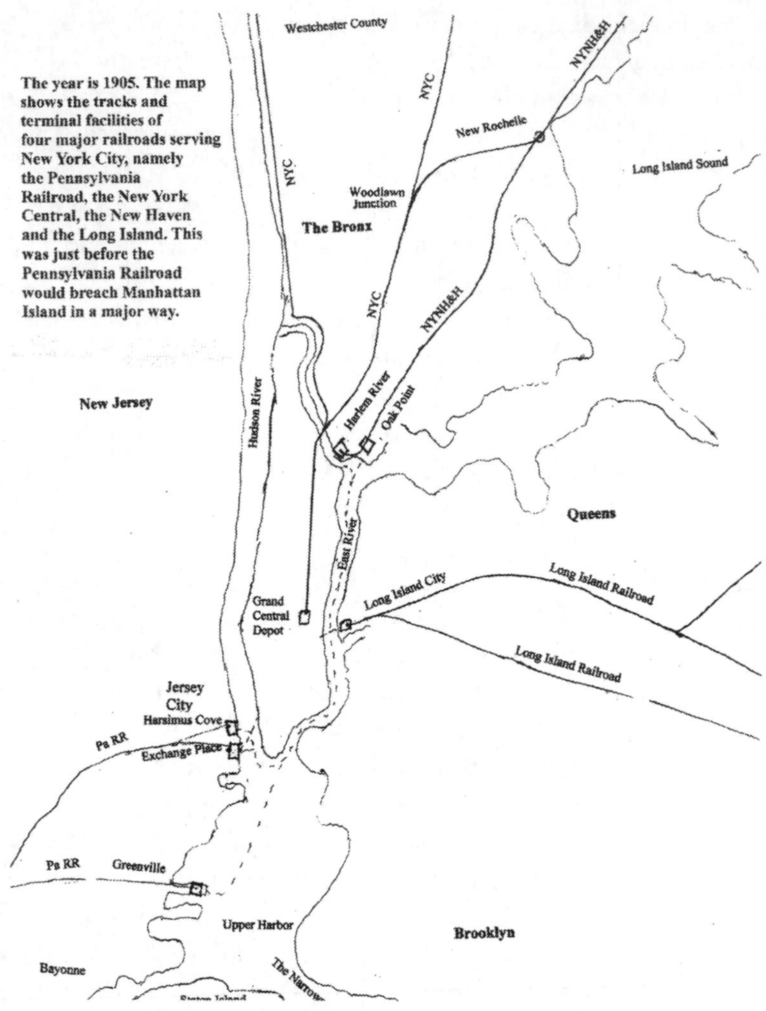

7-4 1905 map of the railroads in and around New York City

The disparity would get worse! Under the gun to electrify its Manhattan operations, the New York Central had announced plans to build a monumental new Grand Central Terminal, one that would be clean and free of all soot and grime. Would the average New Yorker planning a trip to Chicago by sleeping car use the *Twentieth-Century Limited* out of the new Grand Central Terminal or fight his way to a vehicle-clogged ferry for the water transfer to dirty, drafty Exchange Place Station to board the *Pennsylvania Special*? The two stations and their facilities would shout that one railroad had entered the twentieth century while the other was mired in the nineteenth century. The directors of the Pennsylvania Railroad decided, as early as 1901, that they had to establish a passenger station in Manhattan and soon.

Given the new engineering advances in tunneling and the successful use of electric locomotives, the directors decided to build a new line, diverging from the old line at a point about two miles east of Newark, New Jersey. They would establish a station near the diverging point called Manhattan Transfer. The only purpose of this station would be to transfer locomotives, steam to electric, eastward and the reverse westbound. From Manhattan Transfer, the new line would travel on a northeastern route of about five miles and then dive into a three-mile double-track tunnel that would carry the line under Bergen Hill and the Hudson River. The tracks would reemerge at Tenth Avenue and Thirty-First Street in Manhattan, where by a series of ladder tracks the two tracks emerging from the tunnel would fan out into twenty-one tracks, over which they would build a magnificent Manhattan terminal to be known as Pennsylvania Station. Four of the twenty-one tracks would stub end there, with the remaining seventeen tracks continuing east of Pennsylvania Station. Eastbound, once out from under the station, the seventeen through tracks would narrow to four tracks, two under Thirty-First Street and another two under Thirty-Second Street. The eastward tunnels would carry the four through tracks across Manhattan Island, under the East River, and into Long Island City where they would emerge once again into daylight (illustration 7-3). Those four stub tracks under Pennsylvania Station were designed for New Jersey suburban trains that did not need to be restocked before returning to New Jersey. All other mainline trains would not terminate at Pennsylvania Station. Rather, upon arrival from the south or west, the train would discharge passengers, mail, and baggage and then proceed ahead through the East River tunnels and enter a turn-back or balloon track in Sunnyside. Sunnyside had all the facilities for cleaning and restocking the diners, sleepers, and mainline coaches. Unlike Grand Central Terminal, where everything indeed terminated, Penn Station was in part a pass-through station.

The eight northernmost tracks at Penn Station (14-21) were designed for the Long Island Railroad's new fleet of electrified cars off seven branch lines. With tracks 1–4 reserved for the New Jersey commuter trains, this left but nine tracks for the mainline (noncommuter) passenger fleet. The question was whispered, "Did Penn Station have enough track capacity? Should four tracks have been built under the Hudson River instead of two? Should the new station host thirty-one tracks instead of twenty-one?" By contrast, the proposed Grand Central Terminal was being designed to have sixty-seven tracks, forty-one on the upper level and another twenty-six tracks on a lower level. There would be so much room at Grand Central that tenant New Haven could find room for "layup" tracks to store their multiple-unit electric cars and to store most of their through trains as well. Only the New York Central lugged their through trains five miles north to a layup yard at Port Morris (the Bronx), then back again to Grand Central Terminal. As the years have played out, the twenty-one-track capacity of Penn Station has proven to be too small, and a third and fourth Hudson River tunnel is sorely needed. By contrast, the cavernous track capacity at Grand Central Terminal never reached full capacity.

Perhaps the decision not to engineer greater capacity at Penn Station can be excused given the enormous expense of just getting through New York with a gigantic project involving electrification, tunnels, bridges, a station, and a yard (Sunnyside). The Pennsylvania Railroad had the station, tunnels, yard, and electrification ready to go in 1910. The project was a success. The station was an immediate hit, attracting new passengers heading south and west and passengers who no longer had to fight their way over to Exchange Place. Exchange Place would remain in service but mainly for commuters. The Long Island Railroad commuter traffic immediately set new records. Many of these commuters were grateful because they no longer needed to pile on the East River ferry from Long Island City to Thirty-Fourth Street, Manhattan. In 1910, Penn Station was bereft of any direct rapid transit connection, such as Grand Central commuters enjoyed. But this would soon change with the opening of an adjacent subway line in 1916.

The opening of Penn Station and the tunnels in 1910 solved a part of the image problem for the Pennsylvania Railroad. But the need to connect with the New Haven Railroad remained. Thus, the next phase of the giant New York area project began in 1912. The New York Connecting

Railroad project would be next. Beginning at Sunnyside, a two-track railroad would be laid through Queens to a junction with the Bay Ridge freight line. From here, freight trains would have exclusive use of two tracks up and over the Hell Gate Bridge to Oak Point in the Bronx. In addition, from this Queens junction, two more tracks would be laid for the exclusive use of passenger trains. The sheer costs associated with phase one (Penn Station and tunnels) and phase two (Hell Gate Bridge and approaches from Sunnyside and Bay Ridge) left the Pennsylvania Railroad exhausted. Sure, it would have been nice to complete the water barrier removal with a few more touches, such as the Bay Ridge to Greenville tunnel, or two more tunnels under the Hudson or ten more tracks under Penn Station, but for now enough was enough! The two phases were enough to get them started. The rest could wait. Now almost a hundred years later these three missing pieces are still badly needed. Their absence is the subject of intense political debate. Only now most of the needed money will have to be found in the public sector.

For its part, the New Haven Railroad never felt such passenger image problems. After all, the New Haven had been firmly ensconced in Manhattan as early as 1849. Their interest in the Hell Gate Bridge and the New York Connecting Railroad centered about the opportunity to add more business through New York to the south and west and to get rid of those cumbersome and expensive transfer barges. The New Haven directors visualized at least eight daily (each way) passenger trains between Boston and Washington, DC, with another four continuing through to more southern points. Four more trains would ply the rails between Boston and Midwest points, such as Cincinnati, Columbus, Indianapolis, and St. Louis, where they thought they could give the Boston and Albany Railroad a run for its money. Thus, the plan for the great Hell Gate Bridge was to see up to sixteen daily passenger trains in each direction plus ten to twelve freight movements in each direction to Bay Ridge and Greenville. The generous design of the Hell Gate Bridge would permit all of this.

1917–1920

Talk about poor timing! The opening of the Hell Gate Bridge in 1917 could not have come at a worse time! Ordinarily such a massive investment would be put to immediate and intensive use in an effort to recoup the costs. But the congested tracks of both railroads could barely handle the load they were carrying without the added Bridge traffic. In 1917, the two roads somewhat reluctantly reestablished the former boat trains as all-rail Boston–Washington express trains. The *Colonial Express* operated by day, and the *Federal Express* connected Boston and Washington by night. In 1917, the two exhausted partners of Hell Gate Bridge had not even managed to electrify Oak Point to Sunnyside. Steam engines hauled the two trains from Sunnyside to Boston. The two freight tracks over the Bridge were little used in 1917 because the Bay Ridge freight line and docking facilities were not yet completed. New Yorkers of 1917, glancing up at the great structure and seeing so little traffic, wondered why it was built at all.

During the government's operation of the railroad (1918–1920), freight service commenced using steam engines from Oak Point to Bay Ridge. No electrification could take place.

After the War

The dejected New Haven directors knew why all the planned cost savings had gone out the window. The road had to maintain a fleet of steam engines deep in their West End electric zone because the war effort had left the treasury bare and the eighteen-mile electrification of Oak Point–Bay Ridge had to be put on hold. But as the 1920s progressed, finances improved. In 1927, at last, electrification to Bay Ridge was finally completed, and savings as a result of the Hell Gate Bridge could be realized. In 1918, wire was strung from Oak Point over the two passenger tracks of Hell Gate Bridge and on to Sunnyside. Here the overhead wire had to end as the Pennsylvania Railroad and the New Haven Railroad could not agree on AC versus DC power sources.

The Pennsylvania Railroad had not yet committed itself to mainline electrification. Electricity would be used to tow passenger trains over the eleven miles separating Sunnyside and Manhattan Transfer. Low-voltage direct current from third rail, already used on their Long Island Railroad, would do. Passengers traveling between Boston and Penn Station, New York, had to endure two engine changes, one at Sunnyside and another at New Haven.

The 1929 Weekday Schedules

Via the Inland Route or Springfield Line

New York		Boston	Boston		New York
9:15am	Boston Day Exp.	3:30 pm	9:15 am	NY Day Express	3:35 pm
12 Noon	NY–Boston Exp.	6:05 pm	12 Noon	Boston-NY Exp.	6:07 pm
4:02 pm	Twilight Exp.	10:00 pm	4:00 pm	Twilight Exp.	10:07 pm
11:45 pm	Boston Exp.	7:15 am	12 Mid.	NY Express	7:07 am

Via the Midland Route: Boston, Willimantic, Hartford

New York	Boston	Boston	New York
*10:15 am	4:00 pm	6:00 pm	11:40 pm

Via the Shore Line

New York	Boston		Boston		New York
8:25 am	The Mayflower	1:55 pm	8:30 am	The Mayflower	2:00 pm
10:00 am	The Bay State	3:30 pm	*9:00 am	The Colonial	2:50 pm
11:45 am	The New Yorker	5:10 pm	10:00 am	The Bay State	3:30 pm
1:00 pm	The Knickerbocker all parlor car extra fare	6:00 pm	11:45 am	The New Yorker	5:15 pm
1:05 pm	The Shoreliner	6:45 pm	*12:30 pm	The Senator all parlor car extra fare	5:30 pm
*1:35 pm	The Colonial	7:20 pm	1:00 pm	The Knickerbocker all parlor car extra fare	6:00 pm
3:00 pm	The Puritan	8:30 pm	1:05 pm	The Shoreliner	6:40 pm
4:30 pm	The Bostonian	9:55 pm	3:00 pm	The Puritan	8:30 pm

5:00 pm	Merchants Limited all parlor car extra fare	10:00 pm	*4:00 pm	Pittsburgh Exp.	9:55 pm
*5:00 pm	The Senator all parlor car extra fare	10:05 pm	4:30 pm	The Bostonian	9:55 pm
		*4:30 pm to Florida			9:55 pm
6:00 pm	The Gilt Edge	11:25 pm	5:00 pm	Merchants Limited all parlor car extra fare	10:00 p.m
11:30 pm	The Night Express	5:25 am	5:05 pm	The Gilt Edge	10:45 p.m
12:30 am	The Owl nonstop all Pullman cars	6:32 am	*8:00 pm	Federal Express	2:05 am
12:45 am	The Night Hawk nonstop	6:38 am	*10:45 am	The Quaker	5:05 am
*1:00 am	The Federal	7:20 am	11:30 pm	The Night Exp.	5:45 am
*2:05 am	New England Exp.	7:55 am	12 mn	The Owl nonstop all Pullman cars	6:10 a.m

[2]* from Florida 12:35 pm
no departure time stated. Stops at
Penn Station to discharge passengers
only

Inland Route Commentary

Neither the Boston and Albany nor the New Haven management saw any "need for speed." The best of the four Inland Route trains settled back to a thirty-eight-mile-per-hour end-point average speed, slower than in either 1893 or 1910. Further, the disparity between the Inland Route and the Shore Line was growing—both in average speeds and in frequency (illustration 7-1). Both roads published rather relaxed schedules, and only the Boston and Albany kept the charade of giving

2 * indicates a Hell Gate Route bridge train

anemic names (*Twilight Limited, Boston Day Express*, etc.) to their four through trains. The New Haven simply ignored this in their timetables, leaving the trains truly generic and nameless.

The Midland Route Commentary

Miraculously, the old *White Train* route hung on by a thread with one train each way. Curiously the eastbound train was a first-class affair, but with no name. It originated in Philadelphia. It carried a diner and parlor cars. The westbound counterpart ran from Boston to New York, Grand Central Terminal. It departed Boston at 6:00 p.m. Through passengers might have been warned to have an early dinner as this train carried only day coaches.

Shore Line Route Commentary

Between 1916 and 1929, Shore Line frequencies exploded, rising from ten daily trains each way to seventeen or eighteen trains. A part of this increase was due to the opening of the Hell Gate Bridge. The three flyers returned to their five-hour timings of 1910.

Six of the new Boston–New York trains were assigned to the Hell Gate Bridge route for delivery into New York, Pennsylvania Station, and on to points south and west. These trains are noted with an asterisk in the table.

The one or two trains added since 1916 to the Boston–New York Grand Central Terminal route were night trains. The year 1929 would be the high watermark of the overnight Boston–New York market. What in 1910 had been but one overnight train, the *Night Express*, ballooned into six trains. The nonstop and all-Pullman *Owl* followed the *Night Express* plus another nonstop called the *Night Hawk*. Further, that set-out Providence sleeper grew to a solid train of its own (the *Narragansett*) that operated solely between Providence and New York, Grand Central Terminal. Finally two overnight trains operated between Boston and New York Penn Station via the Hell Gate Bridge (the *Federal* and the *Quaker*). Some of this increased overnight travel must have come from passengers who had once used the overnight steamers.

The *Bay State Limited* had its wings clipped. It lost its all-parlor status, gaining day coaches and increased travel times. It was no longer in the exclusive all-parlor car company of the *Knickerbocker Limited* or the *Merchants Limited.*

The Utilization of the Hell Gate Bridge

With the shackles of World War I removed, the directors of the New Haven Railroad were free to add traffic over the great structure and to stretch their reach further south and west of New York City. These new trains would also add to their Boston–New York frequencies. Would we soon see those eighteen daily trains each way over the bridge? Not really! The total passenger traffic each way by the year 1929 was a rather paltry eight trains.

Neither the New Haven nor the Pennsylvania management seemed eager to press their advantage. Rather, after 1920, trains were added slowly. A second Boston–Washington day train came on line, taking some pressure off the *Colonial.* This spiffy new train was to be a five-hour *Shore Line Limited* (replacing the demoted *Bay State*). The all-parlor car *Senator* was established as the daytime leader of the Boston–Washington fleet, joining the original *Federal* and the *Colonial.* A fourth Hell Gate Bridge train, the New York to Philadelphia *Quaker,* took pressure off the *Federal* to handle set-out sleepers at Philadelphia.

To the Midwest and the Deep South via Hell Gate Bridge

A fifth new Hell Gate Bridge train was the experimental *Pittsburgh Express* westbound and its eastbound counterpart, the *New England Express.* The Pennsylvania Railroad figured this would be the train to give those Boston and Albany trains to the Midwest a real run for their money. The westbound Pittsburgh Express left Boston at 4:00 p.m., carrying through-to-Pittsburgh day coaches (a rare concession in the 1920s) plus three sleepers, one to Pittsburgh, one to Cincinnati, and one to St. Louis. A fourth sleeper from Springfield joined the consist at New Haven. Why, that brash New York Central had even invaded the Pennsylvania Railroad stronghold of Pittsburgh with a through Boston sleeper!

These two solid trains were flops. As the table below shows, sheer mileage was working against the Pennsylvania Railroad.

Between Boston and the Midwest

City	via New York Central mileage	via New Haven/Pennsylvania mileage
Boston	0	0
Pittsburgh	605	668
Columbus	716	889
Cincinnati	840	979
Indianapolis	862	1029
St. Louis	1114	1280

The 1929 timetables for the two routes from Boston to the Midwest show the following results:

Westbound

	via New York Central		via New Haven/Pennsylvania (Hell Gate Bridge)
Boston	12:30 pm	2:15 pm	4:00 pm (Pittsburgh Exp.)
Pittsburgh	7:25 am		8:35 am
Columbus	6:15 am		2:40 pm
Cincinnati	8:40 am		5:55 pm
Indianapolis		11:15 am	5:05 pm
St. Louis		5:00 pm	11:30 pm

Eastbound

	via New York Central			via New Haven/Pennsylvania (Hell Gate Bridge)	
St. Louis		9:00 am	Noon	Noon	
Indianapolis		2:00 pm	5:00 pm	5:00 pm	
Cincinnati		3:25 pm	5:30 pm	6:15 pm	
Columbus		6:20 pm	8:35 pm	10:25 pm	
Pittsburgh	5:00 pm			3:07 am	3:40 pm
Boston	10:45 am	12:20 pm	3:20 pm	7:20 pm	7:55 am

Every one of the five Midwest destinations above, even Pittsburgh, was shorter via Albany than via the Hell Gate Bridge. The distance variance was significant, ranging from sixty-three miles at Pittsburgh to 166 miles at St. Louis. How could the Pennsylvania Railroad hope to overcome this, especially since they had mountains to cross instead of a water-level route?

The Pittsburgh Express did manage to beat the Central's time Boston to Pittsburgh, but you couldn't move much west of Pittsburgh before the situation became hopeless. The Central planned to keep matters this way, placing their Boston–Midwest sleepers on prestigious Boston and Albany *name* trains, such as the *Twentieth Century Limited* or the *Southwestern Limited.*

The New Haven–Pennsylvania jointly operated train via the Hell Gate Bridge to Pittsburgh would remain, but the two roads soon agreed any further "through" trains to the Midwest just would not work. No more were tried.

And what of the Boston and south of Washington, DC, market, where up to four trains were once envisioned? In the 1920s, one was tried in cooperation with the Atlantic Coast Line Railroad's *Everglades.* This train was a hybrid, as both the New Haven and the Pennsylvania roads were hedging their bets. The 4:30 p.m. train from Boston was advertised as a new Boston–Florida train. It carried no coaches. There would be a through dining car, a through lounge car, plus sleeping cars for both coasts of Florida. In addition, a Springfield to Miami sleeper was advertised. But why had the New Haven management, so sensitive to properly named trains, allowed this luxurious new entry to go without a name? When Florida-bound passengers arrived at Boston's South Station, the deception was revealed. Their 4:30 p.m. departure carried the name the *Bostonian*, a Boston-Grand Central Terminal express. The no-name Florida cars were simply tacked on the rear where they would stay until Bridgeport, Connecticut, where the train would separate. The *Bostonian* would hustle down the line to Grand Central Terminal, and the no-name Florida train would follow it but diverge to the Hell Gate Bridge to attain Pennsylvania Station, New York. Once in Pennsylvania Station, the abbreviated Boston consist would be filled out with additional sleeping cars and it would now receive its name, the *Everglades.* Eastbound, no such deception occurred. When the eastbound *Everglades* arrived in Penn Station at 6:20 a.m., the New York sleepers were detached, and the Boston section sent on its way, with the abbreviated consist running through to Boston. One sleeper was set out at New Haven for Springfield. This New York to Boston train via the Hell Gate Bridge was not even advertised, perhaps because of its likely erratic schedule after the long trip up from Florida.

The above six Hell Gate Bridge trains would receive two more Bridge companions in the 1920s, neither from Boston. One was the *Montrealor* (northbound) or *Washingtonian* (southbound). This train operated between Montreal, Canada, and Washington, DC, via Hartford and Springfield. The eighth and final Hell Gate Bridge train was the *State of Maine Express* operating between Portland, Maine, and Washington, DC, via Lowell, Worcester, Putnam, and New London.

Highest and Best Use?

Oh, that the directors of the two Hell Gate Bridge railroads of long ago were still alive! We could ask them why they were so reluctant to add the obvious winners—more Boston and Washington, DC, through trains? As it was, they did add one train, the all-parlor car *Senator*. The poor day-coach passenger still had but one available day train, the overcrowded *Colonial,* no different from before the Bridge opened but now all rail with no boat train. Why was one of the eight valuable slots dedicated to a remnant of the *Everglades*, an all first-class train (no coach passengers need apply)? Why did the *Montrealor* (*Washingtonian*) and the *State of Maine Express* follow one another so closely between New Haven and Washington, DC? Why could the Montreal coach passenger find a through car from Washington but not the Maine economy traveler? Why did they expect the Boston–Pittsburgh train with its string of Pullman sleeping cars venturing far into the Midwest would compete with the New York Central and its shorter route?

We believe these flawed decisions were a result of several flawed assumptions. For example, there was the assumption that first-class passengers held the money and that they alone needed pampering. The mass of coach passengers could be left to fend for themselves, riding slower and congested trains, and making several en route transfers. After all, what choice did they have in the 1920s? To mix the classes in, say, one dining car would be déclassé. Another flawed assumption was the belief that western through trains to and beyond Pittsburgh held much promise. Finally there was the assumption that experimental service, such as bringing Maine or Canadian travelers through New York and on to Washington, DC, had to precede any more straight corridor trains, Boston to Washington, DC.

As a result, the New Haven Railroad, after twelve years of experience with passenger trains over the Hell Gate Bridge route, found the great asset badly underutilized. There were just eight weekday trains each way on two tracks over the bridge! The great bridge also held two freight tracks. Not until 1927 did the directors finally electrify these tracks from Oak Point to Bay Ridge, thereby getting rid of those duplicative steam engines. Why the long wait until 1927? Even the relatively minor Danbury branch (twenty-one miles from south Norwalk to Danbury, Connecticut) received electrification in 1925. In 1929, between six and ten freight trains each way were scheduled over the Bridge behind electric locomotives. Thus, there were fewer than twenty total train movements each way daily over the four-track structure.

It began to dawn on the directors that they (or their predecessors) had overdesigned the Great Bridge and underdesigned capacity at Penn Station, New York, and the Hudson River tunnels.

Market Share in 1929

The stock market crash of Friday, October 28, 1929, officially ended the Roaring Twenties. Despite the failure to fully exploit the Hell Gate Bridge, New York-Boston traffic continued to grow through the 1920s. This was especially true of the overnight train market. Frequencies improved but end-point timings were no better than in 1910. The directors fell all over themselves catering to the first-class passengers. The basic needs of day-coach passengers were scarcely considered, with such travelers tolerated with condescension and at times outright disdain. Automobile ownership was increasing rapidly, yet most one-car families viewed the car as something to use locally or close to home. Few drove the rough roads between Boston and New York, preferring to leave the car home for family use. The rental car was still unknown.

By 1929, the New Haven Railroad saw its local and branch line trains surrendering to the automobile. The local trolley companies, so desired in 1905, were no longer in favor. By 1929, most of them were abandoned. Even the New England Steamship Company, the railroad's umbrella subsidiary for the Long Island Sound steamers, had peaked out. A few closed. The more stable, such as the Fall River Line, soldiered on by offering reduced fares.

Despite its problems with traffic loss on branch lines and trolley lines, the New Haven Railroad of 1929 held a solid majority of the Boston–New York business. Still, an observant individual could probably spot a few worrisome clouds on the horizon. A few start-up interstate bus companies were offering a slow, uncomfortable, but cheap travel alternative. Would the much-neglected rail day-coach passenger seriously consider a bus?

Commercial aviation captured the public's attention with Lindbergh's nonstop New York to Paris flight in 1927. The mighty Pennsylvania Railroad and the Santa Fe Railroad were advertising a $267.63 special that could move the traveler from New York to Los Angeles or San Francisco in just two days. They would travel by railway sleepers by night and fly by day (safer by day given the primitive air traffic control system of 1929). No regular Boston–New York service had yet been established.

Should the railroad directors have worried much about bus, airline, or automobile competition in its market? Yes, of course they should have! But as 1929 closed, their collective heads were still in the sand. They reasoned that eighty years (1849–1929) of near complete market domination would probably last forever despite those few intrusive upstarts.

Chapter 8: 1929–1941

The Great Depression and the Looming War

Panics, recessions, and depressions separate the weak from the strong. In good times every railroad seems strong. But bring on a serious downturn, and all the flaws, weaknesses, and past bad judgments reveal themselves. A hefty "rainy day" fund helps as does a brief downturn, but nothing can cover up serious flaws of strategy.

In the earlier years of the Great Depression (1930–1932) the directors of the New Haven Railroad did little. Boston–New York frequencies remained constant as passengers dropped away. Fewer cars were assigned the trains, and that was somewhat welcomed. Those aging Pacific steam engines (4-6-2) were barely able to handle those long strings of steel cars. The Boston and Albany Railroad had the more powerful J-class Hudson steam engines (4-6-4) since 1927. The New Haven directors had failed to upgrade their locomotive fleet when times were good. Further, aging 1913-era steel coaches were still the backbone of the Shore Line fleet as the road entered the Depression.

By 1933, it became clear that prosperity was not "just around the corner." This panic would be deeper, longer, and meaner. The New Haven directors were besieged with more bad news. Their ownership of those electric trolley companies was almost worthless and had to be written off the books. That expensive electric interurban railway, the New York, Westchester and Boston, had actually expanded to Port Chester, New York, in 1929 and was running to the Harlem River Terminal at twenty-minute intervals. Few rode it because few wanted to go to a New York terminal at Willis Avenue and 133rd Streets (Harlem

River). The interurban was having trouble meeting its bond obligations that the New Haven had guaranteed.

Those pampered first-class passengers were dropping away, chastened or ruined by the 1929 stock market crash. Freight revenues were down and branch line passenger business was drying up. The railroad treasury was hemorrhaging. This was one time the directors could not simply cut expenses and wait for the problem to go away.

Two more all-first-class Shore Line flyers bit the dust. By 1938, the *Senator*, first introduced in 1930 as an all-parlor car train, began to accept coach passengers. The other, the *Knickerbocker*, whose stuffy, elitist image now seemed strangely out of place, was removed entirely in 1930 and replaced with an elegant all-parlor-car fast train, the *Yankee Clipper*. In 1938, the *Yankee Clipper* also began to accept coach passengers. The all-Pullman Boston–Florida Everglades train disappeared. The *State of Maine Express* left the Hell Gate Bridge route and Washington, DC, terminating instead at New York's Grand Central Terminal.

Though strapped for funds, the directors of 1933 decided something had to be done about their neglect in providing adequate motive power for the Shore Line trains as well as the need to replace those shabby steel coaches of 1913. A new coach was designed that would feature wider windows and more spacious and comfortable seating, as well as air conditioning. The sleek design of these coaches (illustration 8-1) caught the eye of A. C. Gilbert, the New Haven, Connecticut, toy train manufacturer whose products sold under the name American Flyer. Gilbert mass-produced a toy model of the new coach, and soon the real thing became known as the American Flyer coach. Between 1934 and 1938, the directors took delivery of some two hundred of these cars, thus bumping most of the 1913 cars off the Shore Line. For newer motive power, the directors at last accepted the Hudson-type (4-6-4) steam engine that had proven so successful on the Boston and Albany. Ten of these engines, which were dubbed simply I-5 Shoreline types rather than Hudsons, arrived in 1937 (illustration 8-2).

8-1 An American Flyer coach built in 1935
courtesy of New York, New Haven & Hartford Railroad Photograph Collection, Archives and Special Collections at the Thomas J. Dodd Research Center, University of Connecticut Libraries

In 1934, the New Haven Railroad ordered 205 of these American Flyer cars, enough to completely equip all shoreline trains, including the Hell Gate Bridge route trains. Gone from the main line were any of those 1913-era steel coaches that were hurriedly placed into service when Grand Central Terminal opened. The Pennsylvania Railroad could have matched this replacement of its 1920s-era P-70 steel coaches but instead frittered away its funds on new equipment for its east-west overnight fleet of trains "to ward off any encroachment by the airlines." This gamble failed twice. Commercial aviation continued to attract long-distance travelers who were leaving the railroad. In addition, the Pennsylvania Railroad's prized possession, the northeast

> corridor from New York to Washington, DC, was losing patronage because of shabby and crowded conditions.

The new engines and cars enabled the New Haven Railroad to participate in the great American railway speed up with faster, air-conditioned, and streamlined trains. Suddenly Boston–New York timings, which for twenty-five years had been stuck in the midforties average speed range, shot up to fifty-four miles per hour. The public loved it, and as early as 1937 a minor passenger train renaissance was developing. By the eve of World War II in June 1941, Shore Line frequencies were up but slightly from seventeen to eighteen weekday trains each way. But the small frequency increase masked some bigger changes since 1929. Those experimental Hell Gate Bridge route trains, such as the *Pittsburgh Express*, or the phantom all-Pullman Florida train and the State of Maine Express were gone. Just one survivor remained in that exclusive all-parlor-car extra-fare category, the *Merchants Limited.*

In place of the above removals, management decided to pamper coach passengers and to provide more frequent through service in the purely Boston–Washington, DC, northeast corridor.

The passenger train revival, beginning in 1937, came too late to save the New Haven Railroad from its first bankruptcy in 1935. Debt obligations were coming due with little hope of raising more capital. The trustees of the bankrupt New Haven Railroad lost all interest in more electrification of their main line or electric railways of any kind. Reorganization and survival were the order of the day. Expenses were cut, debt renegotiated, branch-line passenger trains removed, and some line abandonment began. There were two relatively bright spots in an otherwise dismal picture. Traffic on the Shore Line and in the New York City and Boston suburban lines were holding up rather well.

The Boston and Albany Railroad came through the Depression intact, thanks in part to its lessee, the New York Central System. Perhaps the directors of 1894 could feel vindicated. Inland Route trains, although thirty to forty minutes slower than their Shore Line counterparts, retained enough traffic to maintain their full schedule of three trains by day and one by night.

The 1941 Weekday Schedules

Daylight savings time was mandated and in full force when these 1941 schedules were published. Yet railroads adamantly refused to publish "daylight savings time" schedules (except in their suburban timetables). Thus, all times were set for one hour earlier in standard time. The *Merchant Limited's* traditional 5:00 p.m. sailing time was published as 4:00 p.m. standard time, confusing the public but retaining the 5:00 p.m. departure in actual local time.

Via the Inland Route or Springfield Line

Eastbound		Westbound	
New York	Boston	Boston	New York
8:00 am New York-Boston Exp.	1:40 pm	7:05 am	12:50 pm
11:00 am	4:35 pm	11:10 am	4:30 pm
3:00 pm	8:25 pm	3:05 pm	8:45 pm
11:00 pm	6:00 am	11:00 pm	6:33 am

Via the Shore Line

Eastbound			Westbound		
New York		Boston	Boston		New York
7:00 am	The Bunker Hill	11:40 am	7:00 am	Murray Hill	11:45 am
8:00 am	The Mayflower	1:00 pm	* 8:00 am	The Colonial (through Pullman car to Chicago)	1:12 pm
*8:45 am	Penn Bay State	1:40 pm	9:00 am	The Park Avenue	1:35 p.m
9:00 am	The Bay State (combined at New Haven)	1:40 pm	10:00 a.m	42nd St. Express	2:45 p.m
*10:00 am	The Pilgrim (through Pullman car from Chicago)	2:55 pm	* 11:00 am	The Senator features a sun parlor observation car	4:12 pm

11:00 am	The Bostonian	3:45 pm	12 Noon	Yankee Clipper	4:30 p.m
12 Noon	Yankee Clipper	4:30 pm	1:00 pm	New Yorker	5:55 pm
*1:00 pm	The Colonial	5:55 pm	*2:00 pm	The Patriot	6:45 pm
2:00 pm	The Puritan	6:40 pm	2:00 pm	The Puritan (separated at New Haven)	6:55 pm
3:00 pm	The Shoreliner	7:55 pm	*3:00 pm	The Pilgrim	8:05 pm
4:00 pm	Merchants Limited All parlor car extra fare	8:15 pm	4:00 pm	Merchants Ltd. all parlor car extra fare	8:15 pm
*4:00 pm	The Senator features a sun parlor observation car	8:55 pm	4:30 pm	Shore Line Exp.	9:40 pm
5:00 pm	The Gilt Edge	10.00 pm	*5:00 pm	William Penn (through Pullman car to Pittsburgh)	9:40 pm
*6:00 pm	The Patriot	10.40 pm	6:00 pm	Pershing Square	10:35 pm
11:30 pm	The Owl (no coaches)	5:15 am	* 8:00 pm	Hell Gate Exp. (coaches only)	2:00 am
11:45 pm	The Narragansett	5:50 am	*11:00 pm	The Federal	3:48 am
*12:45 am	Hell Gate Express (coaches only)	6:45 am	11:00 pm	The Owl (no coaches)	5:10 a.m
[3]*2:10 am	The Federal (through Pullman car from St. Louis)	7:10 am	11:45 pm	The Narragansett	6:10 a.m

Inland Route Commentary

The great speedup of the late 1930s gave the Inland Route a major boost. Several trains were now averaging forty-three miles per hour in end-point times, which was up from thirty-eight miles per hour in 1929. Thirty to forty-five minutes were cut off most runs. Never before and never since would passengers on the Inland Route enjoy such speed.

3 * indicates a Hell Gate Route bridge train

The five-hour-and-twenty-minute timing of the 11:10 a.m. train from Boston set the pace.

Still, the speedup on the Shore Line left the Inland Route thirty to forty-five minutes slower. Thus, it was no major threat to the Shore Line. Further, neither the Boston and Albany Railroad nor the New Haven Railroad lavished its new equipment on the Inland Route. The American Flyer cars seldom appeared, and those silver-sided Boston and Albany coaches were reserved for travel to Albany and the West. Travelers from Newton, Framingham, and Worcester to New York City could anticipate a few older coaches from both roads retrofitted with air-conditioning but with the same cramped seating. The old diners and parlor cars were retrofitted with air-conditioning.

Thus, while much of the country celebrated the fast, clean, streamlined train, the most the Inland Route was allowed to deliver was "faster than before and air-conditioned." No reporters were down at the station taking pictures of these orphan trains.

Author's collection

Author's collection

8-2 A 4-8-2 Mountain-type and 4-6-4 Hudson-type steam engines on the inland route

For their Inland Route trains between Boston and Springfield, Massachusetts (ninety-eight miles), the Boston and Albany Railroad was well endowed with big, beefy engines, such as the Hudson (4-6-4) from 1929 on the left and the elephant-eared Mountain-type (4-8-2) from 1943 on the right. Timing on those ninety-eight miles was down to 135 minutes with five intermediate stops. With double-track all the way, these engines could keep the Inland fleet on time.

By contrast, until 1937 when the New Haven's I-5 Shoreliner engine (4-6-4) finally arrived, this railroad was embarrassingly short of big beefy engines. The I-4 heavy Pacifics (4-6-2) were the best available but no match for the Boston and Albany's engines of this time.

8-3 A Hudson-type steam engine with Train #6 (Boston and Albany)
Author's collection

Pictured here is a powerful Boston and Albany Hudson-type (4-6-4) engine struggling with Inland Route Train #6 near Lake Quinsigamond. This was the maid-of-all-work local train with a usual consist of eight to ten head-end cars plus two day coaches on the rear. It took seven hours and twenty minutes to cover the two hundred miles between Albany and Boston, making thirty-seven station stops between its end points. It was chronically late. Therefore, few rode it.

8-4 A Boston and Albany Hudson-type engine leaves Trinity Place
Author's collection

By the mid–1930s, the Boston and Albany Railroad increasingly made the Hudson-type engine (4-6-4) their dominant power on the Inland Route. Lighter engines, such as the Pacific (4-6-2) and Ten Wheelers (4-6-0), were phased out. This was in stark contrast to the New Haven Railroad, which initially had nothing heavier than their I-4 Pacifics to power their Shoreline competition. The arrival of the New Haven I-5s in 1937 (Shoreline 4-6-4) helped even the score. Above is a Hudson engine accelerating westbound out of Trinity Place Station. Looking east, the above photo shows two of the three stations, all located within a few blocks of each other. On the right is the Boston and Albany Station from 1896. It was used solely to discharge eastbound passengers. Just beyond the first overpass (Huntington Avenue) and to the right is the New Haven's Back Bay Station. Just east of this point and on the left is the Boston and Albany's Trinity Place Station. None of these structures survive today. In 1969, the Massachusetts Turnpike took title to a strip of land from this area. All three previous stations are now clustered in a new transportation center just east of the bridge along with an easy transfer to the T's Orange Line rapid transit trains.

8-5 An eastbound Boston and Albany Hudson-type engine leaving Huntington Avenue (Back Bay) station
Author's collection

Just east of the Huntington Avenue B & A Station and the Back Bay New Haven Railroad Station, the three tracks of the Inland Route ran side by side with the four-track Shoreline Route. A Boston and Albany Railroad Hudson-type engine is accelerating out of Huntington Avenue Station. The hogger will soon ease off on the throttle as the terminal, South Station, is less than a mile away.

8-6 The *Twilight Limited* westbound at Worcester, Massachusetts
Author's collection

The westbound *Twilight Limited* pauses at Worcester for a drink of water while it loaded passengers. While Worcester is only forty-four miles from Boston, still the Hudson engine probably got its last water about two hours ago at the Brighton Park engine house, some five miles west of Boston. It would have been risky to try to run the next fifty-four miles to Springfield without topping off here at Worcester. Note the predominance of semaphore signals. With the top arm raised, the Twilight has the tower's highball. Contrast the equipment with the Shoreline's American Flier or postwar stainless steel cars used on the New Haven. The Inland Route was the orphan. The Boston and Albany Railroad used its best and newest cars on its so-called east-west overnight fleet with its hand-me-downs going to the Inland Route. Some Inland Route trains did carry a dining car and a parlor car. All regularly-assigned coaches (including the nonreclining variety) were air-conditioned.

8-7 A Boston and Albany Mohawk engine is pulling its train out of Trinity Place Station
Author's collection

In the 1930s, much of the Boston and Albany's Inland Route passenger service was powered by the largest engine available at that time, the Hudson (4-6-4) steam engine. By the late 1930s into World War II, train lengths were growing, putting strain on the Hudson engines, particularly those operating west of Springfield. The answer to the need for heavier power was the L-4 Mohawk (4-8-2). First introduced on the New York Central System in 1943, a few engines from the fifty delivered were rushed to the Boston and Albany to power the heavier east-west trains, such as the Boston sections of the *Ohio State Limited*, the *Knickerbocker*, or the *Southwestern*

Limited. Very few diesel units were assigned to the Boston and Albany Railroad during this period, with numbers twenty-seven and twenty-eight (the *New England States*) being the exception.

8-8 A Boston and Albany Mohawk at North Grafton, Massachusetts
Author's collection

In 1945 near the end of World War II, the New York Central took possession of twenty-five of what many called the ultimate passenger train steam engine, the Niagara (4-8-4). Alas, because of weight and track curvature limitations, those twenty-five engines would not be allowed to operate on the Boston and Albany. Still, the Boston and Albany did gain additional elephant-eared Mohawks that had been bumped off the Water Level Route by the Niagaras. In the illustration, one of these Mohawks races over the Inland Route near North Grafton with the *Southwestern Limited*'s Boston section in tow.

The Midland Route Commentary

The Midland Route, the old New York and New England Railway between Boston and Hartford via Willimantic, died as a through route in the 1930s. Two daily local trains each way still burnished the rails of the old *White Train*, but these were strictly Boston–Hartford trains. There were no parlor cars, no diners, and no advertised through connections. The original "air line" connecting Willimantic and New Haven lost all passenger trains. This, the shortest route between Boston and New York, was a victim of consolidation and its lack of any major population centers between Boston and Hartford.

Shore Line Route Commentary

The *Merchants Limited* once shared its speed and exclusively first-class status with other Shore Line flyers, such as the *Bay State*, the *Knickerbocker*, and the *Senator*. No longer. The *Merchants Limited* was now the exclusive Boston–New York speed leader at four hours and fifteen minutes or a sizzling fifty-four miles per hour average speed over 229 miles. This was a quantum leap over the old record of five hours. The *Merchants Limited* alone carried on the tradition of an all-parlor-car, extra-fare train. The *Yankee Clipper* was anointed the second-fastest train between Boston and New York at four hours and thirty minutes. The balance of the daytime trains stayed between four hours and thirty-five minutes and five hours and twelve minutes.

With eighteen weekday trains each way, the New Haven Railroad management was able to move to a virtual memory timetable. There would be a train every hour beginning at 7:00 a.m. standard time and thence hourly on the hour from each terminal until 6:00 p.m. There was no need to try to remember when the next train departed. Twenty years after these schedules appeared, an airline would use this same technique with devastating results to the rail passenger service.

Strangely, no effort was made to launch really early morning trains that could reach the opposite terminal shortly after the opening of the business day. For example, a 5:30 a.m. departure (local time) from either terminal could be in New York or Boston by 10:00 a.m. Today such early departures are routine. In 1941, the directors considered such early departures as uncivilized and never even tried them. Instead the first morning departures were at 7:00 a.m. standard time or 8:00 a.m. local time, not arriving at the opposite terminal until almost 1:00 p.m. local time. But some business people were abandoning the overnight trains or overnight steamers in favor of an early *flight* the following morning that did get them to their destinations shortly after the business day began. Between 1929 and 1941, two overnight trains were removed. Grand Central Terminal lost one, the all-Pullman *Night Hawk*. Philadelphia lost the other, the *Quaker*. The *Federal*, en route from Washington, DC, could now pick up the relatively few Philadelphia–Boston sleepers since there was no longer enough demand to fill out an entire train.

The dramatic speedup of the Shore Line trains began in 1937. Great enablers were the ten new I-5 Shoreline (4-6-4) steam engines. They had the power to easily handle the longer trains between Boston and New Haven. The rakish, semistreamlined shoreline engines (illustration 8-2) often made three daily one-way trips between Boston and New Haven and covered 80 percent of the total schedule, greatly easing the stress on the underpowered H-4 Pacifics (4-6-2). In June of 1941 the first passenger diesels, the Alco-built DL-109s were still months away from delivery. The Shoreline engines and the American Flyer coaches were the stars. They enabled the New Haven Railroad to equal in quality and beat in quantity the streamlined trains of any other road of this time (illustration 8-9).

8-9 An EP-3 box cab electric engine at Woodlawn Junction
Author's collection

An EP-3 box cab electric engine with a semiexpress from New Haven rolls southbound through Woodlawn Junction. Its pans are down, having just entered the third-rail territory of the New York Central. This heavily riveted engine was introduced in 1931 and lasted almost thirty years in service. During the latter period of chapter 8 (1931–1941) these engines were the backbone of the Shore Line electric fleet.

The Utilization of the Hell Gate Bridge

Eight daily passenger trains each way crossed the great bridge, no different in number than in 1929. However, far more passengers crossed the span in 1941 because at last the trains were going where people wanted to go. Gone were the exotic trains to or from destinations far off the northeast corridor. Gone were any all-first-class trains. Coach passengers were welcomed on all eight trains without restrictions.

By 1941 a durable Hell Gate Bridge route pattern was developing. There would be four Boston–Washington, DC, trains, three by day, and one by night. In addition, there would be two Boston–Philadelphia trains, both by day in 1941. There would be one New York (Penn Station)–Boston mail train that carried rider coaches only. Finally there would be one train that originated in Montreal, Canada (instead of Boston), and terminated in Washington, DC.

Instead of a through train, Pittsburgh and Chicago would have through Pullman sleeping cars from Boston and Springfield. These sleepers would be tacked on to a regular Boston–New York (Penn Station) train and switched to a Pennsylvania Railroad train in New York City. Gone would be any effort to run Boston sleepers through to Cincinnati, Indianapolis, or St. Louis. For the Boston–Florida first-class passenger, there were seasonal (winter) through cars riding behind a regular train. In the summer even these through cars were dropped.

These eight daily trains in each direction were heavy 16–20 car caravans, precluding any speed records. Most were lucky to make the run in five hours. Only the Philadelphia–Boston day trains were relatively short. Clearly a fourth and a fifth Boston–Washington, DC, day train was needed. What held back the two railroads that had that enormous investment in the Hell Gate Bridge? Probably it was squabbles over equipment assignments. In 1941, it was no secret that the New Haven Railroad had the better day coach equipment, particularly those two hundred American Flyer cars. By contrast, the Pennsylvania Railroad had adopted a strategy of reequipping its overnight east-west fleet with the best and newest equipment to the exclusion of its northeast corridor trains. The trains in the New York–Washington, DC, corridor featured old P-70 day coaches from the 1920s, some retrofitted with air-conditioning and some not (illustration 8-10). Why share its best equipment with the Pennsylvania's New York–Washington corridor and get old P-70s for its New England patrons in return? Many authorities believe the Pennsylvania Railroad made a major error in 1937 when they "took for granted" their shorter-haul daytime runs, especially so in the northeast corridor. Just having an electrified railway was not enough. The Pennsylvania Railroad in the corridor, their prized passenger asset, was perceived as shabby, crowded, and undesirable rather than *the standard railroad of the world.*

The all-steel Class P-70 Coach Car of 1907

A class P-70 coach interior dating from about 1910 John H. White, Jr. collection

8-10 P-70 coach interior and exterior

The Pennsylvania Railroad passenger coach was a safe, rugged game changer for the railroads as it accelerated the change from wooden cars to steel. More than one thousand P-70s were built between 1907 and 1929. The driving force for this sudden burst of steel car production was the imminent opening (1910) of the long tunnel approaches into the brand new Penn Station, New York City. With the constant threat of fire, due to derailment, it was considered too risky to permit wooden cars through these tunnels. These cars were almost too durable, many lasting into the 1950s and 1960s. With so many cars coming due for retirement all at once, the Pennsylvania Railroad was overwhelmed with the replacement costs, which they never could fully afford. There was the problem!

The P-70 day coach was designed and mass-produced when railroad management still pampered first-class passengers and relegated the unwashed masses to cramped seating in the P-70s where they traveled in slower trains. In addition to dense seating, many P-70s were never air-conditioned, and very few cars assigned to corridor runs (where they dominated) had reclining seats. The cars were frequently crowded, shabby, and fit poorly in the age of the streamlined train. The P-70 coach also compared poorly to the New Haven Railroad's American Flyer coaches introduced in 1935. From the late 1930s through the 1960s these cars made a mockery of the Pennsylvania Railroad's claim to be *the standard railroad of the world.*

Market Share in 1941

Throughout the 1930s the rail lines slowly lost market share to the automobile. Roads had improved. Some families acquired two cars. Rental cars became available. The diversion of traffic to the automobile was not dramatic. Rather it was a slow but steady erosion of rail traffic.

Commercial aviation came alive in the Boston–New York City market in the 1930s, led by American Airlines. Boston–New York air passengers could choose from some twenty flights each way, with trip times of eighty minutes and a choice of landing at New York's Municipal Airport (later LaGuardia Field) or at Newark, New Jersey, at $11.95 for a one-way trip or $21.50 for a round-trip one. The fare for this one-class service was equivalent to the rail parlor car fares of the time. There was a diversion of some business travelers from rail to air. It was a relatively small diversion but a harbinger of what was coming. The big losers were the overnight sleeper trains, the overnight Long Island Sound steamers, and the all-parlor-car day trains. To many travelers, airplanes were still a bit exotic, perceived as a bit dangerous, unreliable in bad weather, plagued by hard-to-reach terminals, and expensive. The masses would stay with the rail lines for now, while business and government officials who valued time as money made the switch.

Some of the masses did desert to a land alternative cheaper than rail—the bus. Roads improved in the 1930s. Bus trips were longer than rail, but there was convenience in near-to-home stations and rock-bottom fares.

Were it not for the great improvements in rail passenger equipment and speeds introduced in 1937, the market share diversion would have been greater. By June of 1941, rail's share of the Boston–New York market had likely slipped to about 50 percent of all such trips. Rail travel was no longer an overwhelming majority of all travel trips. Long Island Sound steamers were going out of business entirely. The market share winners were the automobile, commercial aviation, and the bus in that order. The looming war would provide a diversion reprieve for the rail lines, leading many in the rail industry to believe their loss of market share had come to an end.

Chapter 9: 1941–1947

World War II and Postwar Rail Passenger Euphoria

As the railroads entered World War II, the Shore Line dominated the Boston–New York travel market. The Midland Route was gone as a through line, and the Boston and Albany's Inland Route (Springfield Line) was a fading orphan.

As freight and passenger traffic kept building in 1941, the New Haven Railroad trustees were determined to keep their road fluid. Undue congestion could only lead to another government takeover as it did in World War I. As early as 1940 the trustees recognized that their steam motive power, save for those I-5 Shoreline engines, was getting old. Rather than order newer steam engines, they placed a prewar order with locomotive builder ALCO for ten DL-109, two-thousand-horsepower diesel electric units. These ten units could haul passenger or freight trains. They were usually paired, producing five dual-purpose locomotives of four thousand horsepower each. The DL-109s were needed at once. The US War Production Board approved an order for fifty more units with delivery strung out through the 1942–1945 period. This was just enough to pull the New Haven Railroad through the war.

Almost all Shore Line passenger trains had a modern engine leading between Boston and New Haven. The electric engine fleet was sufficient for all traffic west of New Haven. In this 1941–1947 period the Shore Line passenger traffic frequency hit an all-time high of twenty-one eastbound trains and twenty westbound trains. The prewar growth of automobile travel was halted because of the rationing of tires and gasoline. Commercial aviation also had wartime restrictions. Passengers were back on the trains almost like it was 1910 all over again. Every train was full. Every piece of equipment, old or new, was out on the road. Space in parlor and sleeping cars became scarce.

The frequency tables that follow (illustration 9-2) show only the scheduled twenty or twenty-one daily weekday trains between Boston and New York. What they do not show are the frequent "second sections" of certain trains or troop trains, particularly on the Hell Gate Bridge route. This war-induced surge bolstered the spirits of the trustees. With a positive cash flow and profitable once again, the trustees could plan for the end of bankruptcy with a solid reorganization plan. They could also address capital needs such as reequipping the passenger-car fleet (illustration 9-1) and retiring aging steam engines, replacing them with the modern diesel-electric locomotives.

9-1 New cars for the New Haven after World War II (1947) Courtesy of New York, New Haven & Hartford Railroad Photograph Collection, Archives & Special Collections at the Thomas J. Dodd Research Center, University of Connecticut Libraries

Passenger coach #8695 was one of 250 streamlined cars ordered in 1947 to completely equip the Shoreline with the latest and the best.

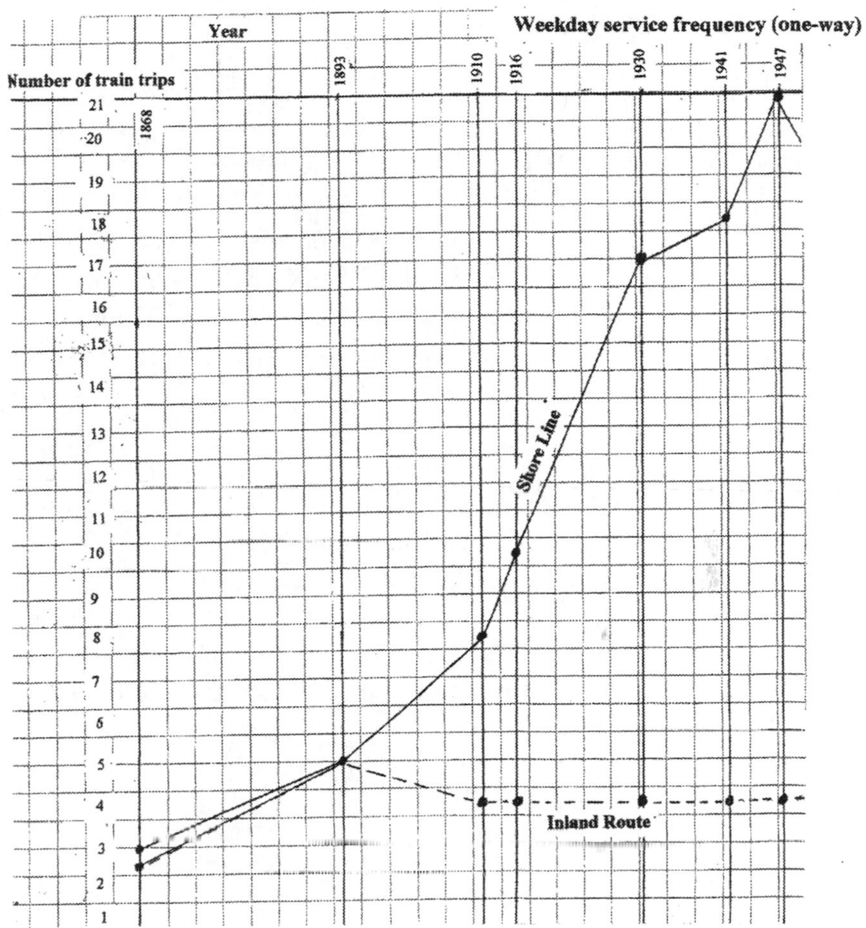

9-2 Weekday service frequency, 1868 to 1947

The 1947 Weekday Schedules

The following schedules were published for the summer of 1947 and are stated in *standard time*, one hour slower than the prevailing daylight savings time.

Via the Inland Route or Springfield Line

New York	Boston	Boston	New York
Eastbound		Westbound	
7:20 am	1:35 pm	7:00 am	1:00 pm
11:30 am	5:15 pm	11:00 am	4:56 pm
3:10 pm NY–Boston Exp.	8:45 pm	3:20 pm	9:05 pm
11:10 pm	6:25 am	10:00 pm	5:55 am

Inland Route Commentary

Three trains by day and one by night continued a frequency pattern first begun in 1910. No additional trains were added during World War II. The morning and midday trains needed from five to thirty additional minutes between end points compared to 1941. The very best Inland Route end time of five hours and twenty minutes, achieved in 1941, slipped to five hours and thirty-five minutes (illustration 9-3). At first blush this added time could appear to be the result of war traffic volume. However, by 1947 most of this time padding was gone from the Shore Line. A closer look revealed something else was at work here.

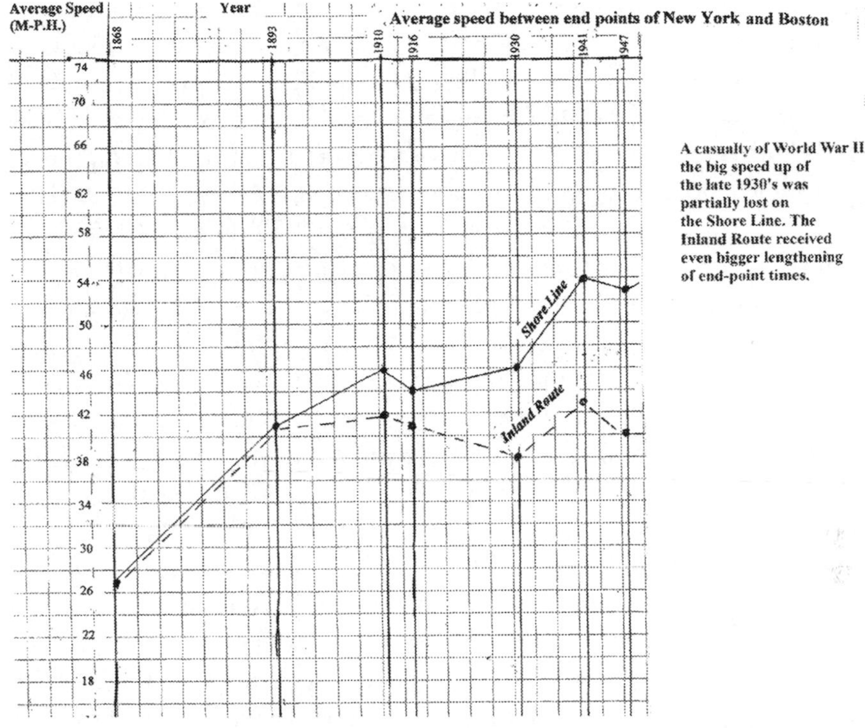

9-3 Weekday average speed, 1868 to 1947

> The Springfield Line since 1937 had the oldest hand-me-down equipment off both the New Haven and the Boston and Albany Railroads. These orphan trains were unloved by New Haven management, which was quite willing to keep Springfield Line well subordinated to its exclusively owned Shore Line Route. The Boston and Albany, in its defense, had valiantly tried to compete with the Shore Line by offering fast trains over its ninety-eight miles between Boston and Springfield. But between Springfield and New York City, these through trains languished under New Haven Railroad control, burdened as they were with numerous stops and heavy head-end traffic.

Although they didn't come right out and say so, the Boston and Albany officials had all but given up on their Springfield Line route by 1947. The evidence for this is in the schedules of the morning and midday eastbound trains from New York to Boston. In previous schedules the Boston and Albany kept in Springfield a dedicated crew and equipment for the exclusive purpose of hauling these solid trains from Springfield to Boston. But by 1947, these dedicated resources were removed. Now eastbound trains would have their coaches and parlor car removed at Springfield and added to the rear of an existing Albany–Boston train. Thus, the 7:20 a.m. from New York (train #50) might languish in Springfield for an hour or more, awaiting the chronically late Boston and Albany Train #64, the *Water Level Limited* from Chicago and St. Louis. The scheduled twenty-minute layover in Springfield could just as well be an actual two hours. Similarly the 11:30 a.m. train from New York (Train #54) had a scheduled twelve-minute connection with Boston and Albany Train #10, the Mohawk from Chicago. The long-distance eastbound Boston and Albany trains were notoriously unreliable.

The Westbound morning and midday trains from Boston also lost their dedicated crew and equipment, but there was little impact on the schedule because westbound Boston and Albany trains generally ran on time. Only the afternoon Inland Route trains (#558 and #559) were spared this economy move because they carried sufficient traffic to warrant a dedicated crew and locomotive for a solid train. Needless to say, traffic on the Inland Route dropped since two of its four eastbound trains became unreliable. New York–bound passengers from Framingham and Worcester saw their service downgraded, while Shore Line patrons were enjoying unprecedented service frequencies and speed. The management of the New Haven and Boston and Albany roads seemed not to care, the first whiff of indifference that would eventually engulf both roads.

Via the Shore Line Route

Eastbound			Westbound		
New York		Boston	Boston		New York
6:00 am	Roger Williams	10:40 am	6:00 am	Roger Williams	10:33 am
7:00 am	Murray Hill	11:50 am	7:00 am	Murray Hill	11:45 am
8:00 am	Mayflower	1:00 pm	*8:00 am	The Colonial	1:10 pm
9:00 am	Bay State	1:45 pm	9:00 am	Bay State	1:35 pm
*9:00 am	William Penn	1:55 pm	10:00 am	42nd St. Express	2:40 pm
10:00 am	The Pilgrim	2:55 pm	*11:00 am	The Senator	4:12 pm
11:00 am	The Bostonian	3:45 pm	12:00 noon	Yankee Clipper	4:30 pm
12.00 Noon	Yankee Clipper	4:30 pm	1:00 pm	The New Yorker	6:10 pm
*1:00 pm	The Colonial	6:00 pm	*2:00 pm	The Patriot	6:45 pm
2:00 pm	The Puritan	6:45 pm	3:00 pm	The Pilgrim	8:05 pm
3:00 pm	The Shoreliner	7:55 pm	4:00 pm	Merchants Ltd. extra fare—all parlor car	8:20 pm
4:00 pm	Merchants Limited extra fare—all parlor car	8:20 pm	4:05 pm	The Gilt Edge	8:45 pm
*4:00 pm	The Senator	9:10 pm	*5:00 pm	William Penn	10:00 pm
5:00 pm	The Gilt Edge	10:05 pm	6:00 pm	Pershing Square	10:50 pm
*6:00 pm	The Patriot	10:50 pm	7:00 pm	The Commander	11:40 pm
7:00 pm	The Commander	11:45 pm	*8:00 pm	Hell Gate Exp.	1:50 am
11:30 pm	The Owl sleeping cars only nonstop	5:15 am	*10:00 pm	The Federal	2:53 am
11:45 pm	The Narragansett	5:50 am	*11:05 pm	The Quaker	4:30 am
*12:30 am	Hell Gate Express	6:30 am	11:30 pm	The Owl sleeping cars only nonstop	5:10 am
*1:35 am	The Quaker	6:45 am	11:45 pm	Narragansett	6:00 am
[4]* 2:10 am	The Federal	7:10 am			

Midland Route Commentary

The Midland Route died as a through route in the 1930s. Not even the traffic surge of World War II could revive it. The two isolated

4 * Indicates a Hell Gate Route bridge train

Boston–Hartford regional trains soldiered on as thin reminders of what had once been.

Shore Line Route Commentary

With the demise of the Midland Route and the downgrading of the Inland Route, it fell to the Shore Line to provide the good news. In frequency, 1947 was the high watermark in almost ninety years of through Boston–New York City Shore Line service. The eighteen weekday trains of 1941 grew to an astonishing twenty westbound and twenty-one eastbound trains. In comparing 1947 with the splendid schedules of 1941, patrons still had hourly departures on the hour from 6:00 a.m. through 7:00 p.m. The trip times had been lengthened by a modest five to ten minutes because of heavy wartime loadings. The *Quaker* was restored as an overnight Boston–New York–Philadelphia train. An additional Grand Central Terminal–Boston schedule (the *Commander*) filled out the day schedule. The *Merchants Limited* was the flagship train, still all-parlor and extra fare and still the fastest at four hours and twenty minutes.

The Utilization of the Hell Gate Bridge

The great buildup in Shore Line frequency eluded the Hell Gate Bridge Route, which continued with its 1941 schedule of just eight trains each way.

These eight trains were groaning with passengers who were packed into twenty-car trains and often operated in two sections. The New Haven Railroad dutifully supplied these trains with their best available equipment, including the air-conditioned American Flyer coaches. The Pennsylvania Railroad continued its policy of placing its newest cars on its overnight east-west trains and equipping its share of the Hell Gate Bridge trains with the ancient, cramped P-70 coaches from the 1920s. This painful equipment disparity left the New Haven Railroad less than anxious to increase much-needed frequencies over the Hell Gate Bridge, where its superior cars would be swallowed up between New York and Washington, DC.

The directors of the 1947 Pennsylvania Railroad felt their railroad was most vulnerable to traffic erosion on its overnight east-west fleet, where commercial aviation was making inroads. With new equipment, they reasoned they could hold on to most of this traffic. They felt patrons along the Northeast Corridor were less apt to defect to commercial aviation because of the relatively short runs and abundant frequencies. Once the east-west fleet was upgraded, they could then turn to upgrading their Northeast Corridor equipment. Events would prove the directors wrong on all counts. The east-west overnight traffic began to shrink further just as the new equipment arrived. Disgruntled passengers in the heavily traveled Northeast Corridor were more than ready for an aviation alternative, which was becoming more and more convenient. The Pennsylvania Railroad treasury ran dry before the directors were able to put more than a dent in their plans to reequip their aging equipment. As a result, their huge investment in the Hell Gate Bridge languished, not for lack of willing patrons but for lack of good judgment.

None of the eight trains crossing the great bridge (including the Montrealor/Washingtonian) ventured off the northeast corridor south of New York City. A bare vestige of the old Boston–Pittsburgh solid train remained in the form of a through Boston sleeping car off the *William Penn* westbound and the *Quaker* eastbound.

Market Share in 1947

The rail lines entered World War II with an estimated 50 percent of all through travel between New York and Boston. This percentage share remained constant throughout the war and for at least an additional year, thanks in part to restrictions on the use of automobiles and on commercial aviation. The percentage was probably a bit higher during the peak years of 1943 to 1945 and had begun to slip by the end of 1947.

Never before had rail moved so many people over this route. Howard S. Palmer, the New Haven's lead trustee, would see the railroad reorganized and freed of trustee management (bankruptcy) in October 1947. A new board of directors, happy with his stewardship as trustee, promptly elected Palmer president of the newly privatized railroad. Then the directors went on a spending spree, ordering some 250 new stainless steel coaches, parlor cars, dining cars, grill cars, and sleepers. This would be enough equipment to assure all main-line trains had modern, air-conditioned cars. The older heavyweight parlor cars, sleepers, and dining cars would be replaced. About the only place where a car would not be air-conditioned would be on suburban commuter trains.

Additional diesel-electric locomotives were ordered too. When they arrived in the early 1950s, steam engines would be just a memory.

The suburban fleets in both New York City and Boston were aging, but most new equipment here would have to wait. In 1947, the directors placed an order for a hundred multiple-unit electrics for suburban service between Grand Central Terminal and Stamford, Connecticut (illustration 9-4). It was a start. The directors were proud of their main-line service and felt they would retain their share of the market into the postwar years given the new equipment on order. Near euphoria reigned in the boardroom. The New Haven Railroad had ceded purely local and branch-line traffic to the automobile, but the New York-Boston market would remain their oyster. It just made so much sense, but it was not to be.

9-4 A new suburban electric multiple unit car
#4464 from 1954
Courtesy of New York, New Haven & Hartford Railroad Photograph Collection, Archives & Special Collections at the Thomas J. Dodd Research Center, University of Connecticut Libraries

The suburban fleet of multiple-unit electric cars had not seen a new unit since the early 1930s. This fleet was sizable, numbering an active but aging roster of about 250 cars. In 1952, the directors of the New Haven Railroad made a start in replacing them with an order for a hundred new cars, one of which is pictured here. They featured air-conditioning, soft, high-backed seats, and fluorescent lighting. Delivery began in 1954. All of these cars were retired by 1986.

9-5 The 1949 diesel-powered *New England States*, #27

Author's collection

The initial Boston and Albany *New England States* (#27 and #28) were introduced in 1937 as a new train replacing the Boston Section of the *Twentieth Century Limited*. The *States* used the best of the hand-me-down equipment off the newly streamlined *Twentieth Century*. By 1948, the *States* was ready to regain its stature as the flagship train of the Boston and Albany. It is pictured above in 1949, traversing the Inland Route with its new EMD diesels and equally new streamlined and silver-sided cars from Pullman-Standard (Worcester plant). Oh, that the Inland Route's Boston–New York City trains should look like this!

Author's collection

As late as 1947 and 1948, the only diesel engines regularly assigned to the Boston and Albany fleet were the EMD F units. Steam ruled most other passenger train movements. These F units powered trains #27 and #28, the *New England States*. Illustrations 9-5a and 9-5b are two shots of the F units in action. 9-5b shows Train #27 approaching Worcester.

9-6 A new Alco PA pulls the *Yankee Clipper* out of Boston, 1948
Author's collection

With new Alco PA units up front and shiny new cars from Pullman-Standard (except for the grill car), this 1948-era *Yankee Clipper* is a class act. The Shoreline was beginning to overshadow the Inland Route, which still operated older equipment and steam engines spewing smoke, soot, and hot cinders.

9-7 An Alco DL 109 still rated top assignments in 1949 Author's collection

9-8 An Alco DL 109 approaches South Station Author's collection

These Alco DL 109 units saw heavy use during World War II. After the war they soldiered on for another six or seven years. Above is a pair leading a Shoreline Route Express out of South Station and soon to arrive in Back Bay. In these immediate postwar years, Shoreline Express trains also were led by steam powered I-5 (Shoreline) engines and Alco PAs

These DL 109s have almost completed their Shoreline run as they leave Back Bay Station (visible just behind the overhead bridge) and run off the remaining mile to South Station.

9-9 An Alco PA between Back Bay and South Station
Author's collection

An almost new Alco PA 0782 struts its stuff in 1948 as it nears Boston's South Station with the *Bay State* #10.

9-10 Long Island RR Engine #4
out on the street at Bay Ridge
Author's collection

9-11 Long Island RR Engine #4
in the yard at Bay Ridge
Author's collection

Shunter engine no. 4, pictured here in 1944, was owned and operated by the Long Island Railroad. Whereas the Bay Ridge Yard itself was electrified for the New Haven engines, the industrial tracks on the adjoining Brooklyn streets were the province of No 4.

The New Haven Railroad used their electric locomotives to move freight traffic over the Hell Gate Bridge and over the nineteen-mile trek beginning at Oak Point (the Bronx) and thence across the Hell Gate Bridge and through Queens and Brooklyn to the Bay Ridge (Brooklyn) Yard on the waterfront. From here the freight cars were barged across the Upper New York Harbor to the New Jersey side. Most cars went to the Pennsylvania Railroad in the Greenville section of Jersey City. Ownership across these nineteen miles was complex. North of Oak Point, the tracks were owned solely by the New

Haven Railroad. Between Oak Point and Fresh Pond Junction (Queens), trackage was owned by the New York Connecting Railroad (a joint New Haven–Pennsylvania Railroad Corporation). South of Fresh Pond Junction and across all of Brooklyn to the Bay Ridge Yard, the right-of-way was owned by the Long Island Railroad. The water crossing to Greenville used New Haven tugs and barges but also leased Pennsylvania Railroad equipment.

9-12 New Haven electric engines at the sand dome in Bay Ridge
Author's collection

Several New Haven Railroad electric motors (EF-1s) refill their sand domes in Bay Ridge, Brooklyn, in wartime 1944. One of the giant Bush Terminal warehouses creates a backdrop.

9-13 A Boston and Albany Mohawk type engine nears Boston
Author's collection

A Mohawk engine leads Boston and Albany Train #6, the local from Albany, toward its terminal in Boston. It has just pulled out of Huntington Avenue. It's running late. Not even this massive steam engine can keep #6 on schedule, given what it faces en route, namely frequent and often lengthy station stops.

9-14 The Woodlawn Junction Plant in 1943
Author's collection

A look at the Woodlawn Junction Plant during wartime 1943. On the left, a New York Central Railroad MU from North White Plains nears Woodlawn Station, where a small group awaits to board. Meanwhile, a New Haven Railroad MU from Grand Central Terminal moves across the plant to its home rails. Within a minute, third rail shoes must be folded up and pantographs raised.

9-15 Boston and Maine Railroad at Salem, Massachusetts
Author's collection

Taking the seventeen-mile trip from Boston out to Salem, Massachusetts, was a popular excursion in this period. Salem tour operators met the trains and entertained the curious visitors by showing them the structures, the cemeteries, and the hills, all relics of the 1692 *witchcraft trials* in which nineteen alleged witches were condemned and executed. The railroad figured what better way to greet the tourists than with this brooding, castlelike station. Let their imagination visualize witches flying between the turrets.

To reduce the presence of the Boston and Maine Railroad on Salem's main business street, the railroad went underground for a half of a mile just north of the station. This was the line of the old Eastern Railroad, which was double-track except for this tunnel section. In the picture, a southbound train moves off the tunnel's single track, while a northbound train waits in the station for clearance.

9-16 Engine #4265 moves its train northbound out of Salem, Massachusetts
Author's collection

Once the southbound train cleared off the single track, the northbound train could be released. Today the castle station is gone. The station itself has been downsized and relocated to the tunnel's north end. It now carries commuter trains (the T) for Newburyport and the Gloucester Branch (Rockport).

Chapter 10: 1947–1957

Market Share Slips as the Railroad Tries to Reinvent Itself

Boston–New York passenger traffic held up quite well during the first half of the 1947–1957 period. The New Haven Railroad took delivery of its new 250-car fleet of stainless steel passenger cars. By 1950, every Shore Line train had some brand-new equipment. The flagship train, the *Merchants Limited*, was at its finest—all stainless steel parlor cars, plus a new diner and a tavern observation lounge. The *Merchants* end-point times shrank to just four hours, for an average speed of fifty-seven miles per hour, the best yet recorded. The *Yankee Clipper* followed with a classy timing of four hours and fifteen minutes. The balance of the Shore Line fleet had some time clipped off of their 1947 schedules. In the 1947–1952 period an occasional stainless steel coach even ran through from Boston to New York via the Springfield Line, but alas, no effort was made to accelerate trains on the Inland Route.

After 1952, the rail line passenger fortunes headed downhill. In fact, the economic fortunes of the New Haven's entire freight and passenger network worsened. How disappointing this must have been after the massive equipment purchases and service speedups. The fickle passengers were deserting to the private automobile. Car drivers could now race down the Connecticut Turnpike virtually alongside the trains. For many miles the turnpike took one entire side of the railroad right-of-way, leveling many a railroad-served industry in the process. The turnpike attracted trucks too. Those overnight Boston to Philadelphia and Baltimore freight trains (the Speed Witches) could compete with trucks before the superhighway. Now the truckers, unfettered with barge transfers, could beat the rail freight trains. The railroad's shorter-haul, high-value northeast corridor freight business was under attack. So too were the New England mills' valued rail customers, whose owners were closing them and moving south in favor of cheaper labor.

The Shore Line passenger trains were beginning to lose money. For all of their frequency and speed, these trains were labor intensive, especially the dining cars and grill cars. When the trains were full, the railroad could eke out a profit. But as patronage fell off and food expenses didn't, those small profits turned to losses.

By 1953, the New Haven Railroad was in trouble. Those heady forecasts of 1947 never materialized. The directors began changing presidents (Palmer, Dumaine, Dumaine Jr., McGinnis, Alpert) every several years in the belief that the right one could turn things around.

The revolving presidents, especially McGinnis and Alpert, believed they had to get passenger train costs under control. They went further, believing the stodgy, full-service train was a relic of the past and needed a major change with a new image. They were easy targets for the mid–1950s salesmen of lightweight trains in the form of the Dan'l Webster or the John Quincy Adams, both Talgo trains. In addition, there was the Roger Williams, a stylized set of rail diesel cars. All initially lacked any dining facilities or first-class parlor cars (illustration 10-1). The directors were led to believe that passengers would willingly give up the solid ride of a standard-truck car and a comfortable diner for lightweight, noisy, and flimsy little cars with no first-class amenities or food service. The public was sold the sizzle of stylish image and speed. These little trains were carded with end-point times of between four and four and a half hours, equaling or beating the *Merchants Limited.* In the summer of 1957, three of these "new image" trains bumped the stodgy old trains. The results were disastrous. The new image service was regarded as unreliable (frequent breakdowns), uncomfortable, and very forgettable. Within two years of their introductions, each was removed from main line service. Several were reassigned to shorter runs, such as New York–Springfield.

10-1 The Three Experimental Lightweight Trains

The John Quincy Adams
Photo courtesy of New Haven Railroad Historical & Technical Association Inc. Collection

From a Fairbanks–Morse ad that appeared on the inside front cover of the January 1957 issue of *Trains*

The Roger Williams
Photo courtesy of New Haven Railroad Historical & Technical Association Inc. Collection

From a Budd Company ad for its new generation of custom-made trains

The Dan'l Webster
Kodachrome by William T. Clynes
Photo courtesy of New Haven Railroad Historical & Technical Association Inc. Collection

NH #3001 and the Dan'l Webster leave Providence Union Station westbound on April 11, 1957.

President Patrick McGinnis ordered three experimental high-speed passenger trains during 1955. One of these trains, the *Dan'l Webster*, seen here at Providence, Rhode Island, on April 11, 1957, was a Pullman Train X powered by push-pull Baldwin–Lima–Hamilton RP-210 locomotives.

These lightweight trains failed to deliver what the public wanted, and this hurt the railroad's image, particularly with business travelers. The fixed consist of these trains made it impossible to add cars when the demand was there.

The 1957 Weekday Shore Line Schedules

Eastbound		Westbound			
New York		Boston	Boston		New York
7:30 am	The Mayflower (lightweight train)	11:30 am	7:10 am	The Murray Hill (lightweight train)	11:30 am
8:00 am	The Murray Hill	1:05 pm	8:00 am	The Mayflower	12:05 pm
10:00 am	The Bay State	2:40 pm	*8:30 am	The Colonial	1:30 pm
*10:30 am	William Penn	3:10 pm	10:00 am	The Bay State	2:30 pm
12:00 noon	The Bostonian (lightweight train)	4:15 pm	*11:00 am	The Senator	3:30 pm
1:00 pm	Yankee Clipper	5:15 pm	12 noon	42nd St. Express	4:45 pm
*2:00 pm	The Colonial	6:45 pm	1:00 pm	Yankee Clipper	5:15 pm
3:00 pm	The Puritan	7:30 pm	2:00 pm	The New Yorker (lightweight train)	6:15 pm
*4:00 pm	The Senator	8:30 pm	*3:00 pm	The Patriot	7:30 pm
5:00 pm	Merchants Ltd.	9:05 pm	4:00 pm	The Gilt Edge	8:55 pm
6:00 pm	The Gilt Edge	10:45 pm	5:00 pm	Merchants Limited	9:05 pm
*7:00 pm	The Patriot	11:50 pm	*6:00 pm	The William Penn	11:10 pm
8:00 pm	The Commander (lightweight train)	12:15 am	8:00 pm	The Commander (lightweight train)	12:00 mid.
12:30 am	The Owl (all sleeping cars)	6:20 am	*8:45 pm	The Pilgrim	2:10 am
12:45 am	The Narragansett	6:50 am	*11:00 pm	The Federal	3:35 am
*2:25 am	The Quaker (carries a sleeper and a coach from Pittsburgh)	7:45 am	*11:50 pm	The Quaker	5:30 am
[5]*3:10 am	The Federal	8:25 am	12:30 am	The Owl	6:15 am

Inland Route Commentary

In 1952, the Inland Route (Springfield Line) joined the Midland Route by offering no through Boston–New York trains, thus ending a tradition of almost a hundred years. In the late 1940s, the Boston and Albany Railroad became enamored with those RDC or self-propelled

5 *Indicates a train that operates via Hell Gate Bridge

raid diesel cars that they called Beeliners. Management's strategy was to cut passenger train costs and to try to grow the passenger business by offering record speeds and frequencies with those little, one, two and three car trains (illustration 10-2). Trip times over the ninety-eight-mile Boston-Springfield route shrank to just two hours. With five intermediate stops and plenty of hills and curves, the jaunty forty-nine-miles-per-hour average speeds were impressive and have never been equaled since. By 1957, the Boston and Albany east-west fleet of trains each way had shrunk to just five trains. Everything else was rail diesel cars or purely suburban trains. Costs were lowered, and there was a modest improvement in total passenger loadings, which would last until the parallel Massachusetts Turnpike opened in 1964, whereupon automobiles and buses attacked the gains.

10-2 A Budd RDC self-propelled diesel car
Photo by Bevis R. W. King

> The New Haven Railroad made extensive use of the Budd Rail Diesel Car. There were forty such cars in service in the 1950s and 1960s. Dubbed Shoreliners, these self-propelled cars saw service on branch lines and in commuter service in the Boston region.

The Inland Route night train between New York and Boston was withdrawn, including the Springfield and Worcester set-out sleepers. While it was still possible to travel between Boston and New York via the Inland Route, a part of the trip would have to be in a diesel rail car with a change in Springfield. The Boston and Albany and the New Haven Railroads did coordinate their schedules in Springfield, but with no new through speed records set and no first-class amenities present.

The directors of the New Haven Railroad recognized the "change in Springfield" mandate made the Boston and Albany vulnerable at Worcester, the Commonwealth's second largest city. If the Worcester–New York traveler had to change trains, why not ask him to make the change in New London? In a direct grab for the Worcester business, the New Haven began a seventy-two-mile branch-line shuttle between Worcester and New London using diesel rail cars. These shuttles were dubbed Shoreliners (illustration 10-2). One train set would be sufficient for the two scheduled round trips. Now the Worcester–New York City traveler had a choice of two ways to go—the traditional Inland Route via Springfield (Beeliner) or via New London (Shoreliner). Now no matter how you left Worcester by train, you were like a branch line passenger aboard a Spartan rail diesel car with the need to change to the "big, real train" somewhere en route.

Shore Line Commentary

In comparison to 1947, the 1957 schedules removed four eastbound and three westbound frequencies (illustration 10-3). The flagship *Merchants Limited* lost its all-first-class status. Coaches plus new stops at Route 128 and New London lengthened end-point times to a still-respectable four hours and five minutes (illustration 10-4). Over the thirty-year period from 1927 to 1957, the New Haven Railroad completely changed its attitude toward coach passengers. In 1927, coach passengers rode the slower trains in cramped cars. Elegant, all-first-class flyers set the style and speed records. By 1957, only the eastbound *Owl* would accept no coach passengers.

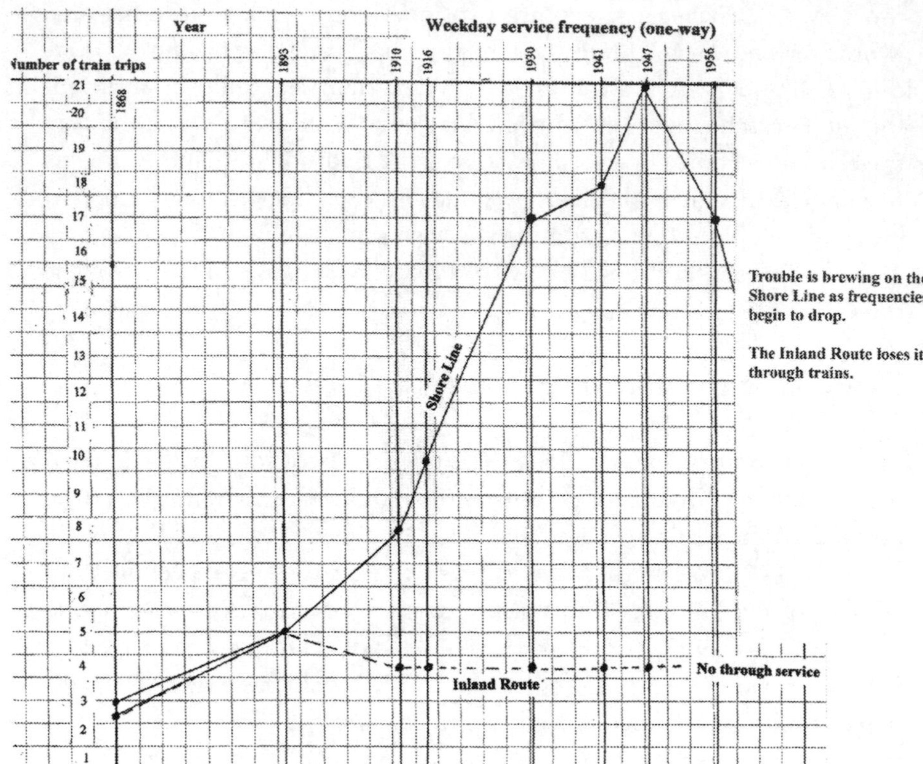

10-3 Weekday service frequency in 1956

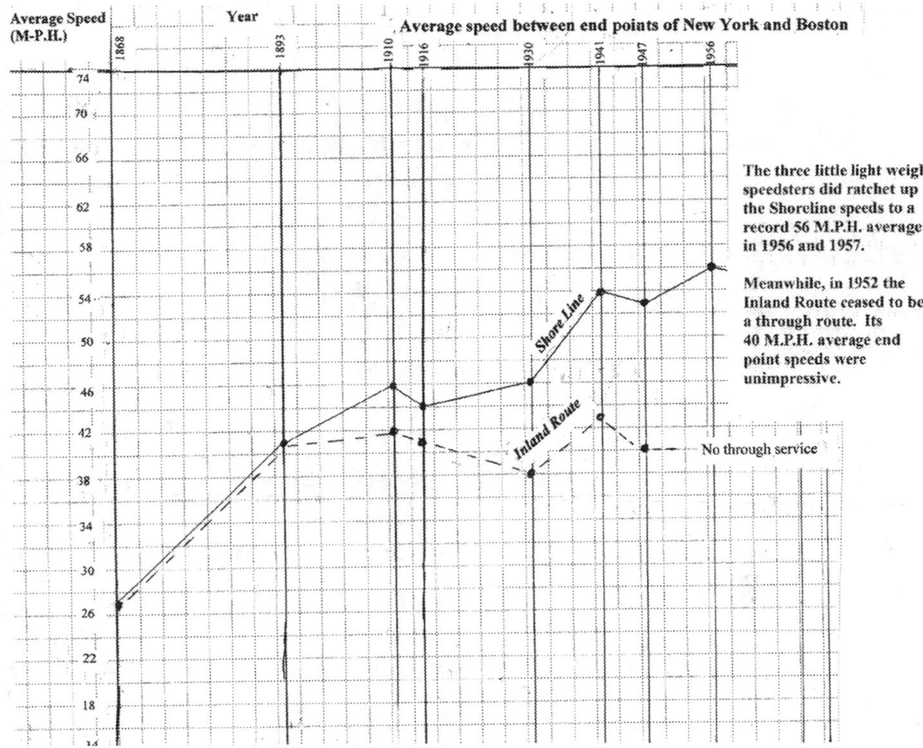

10-4 Average speeds to 1956

The night trains held up reasonably well too. Evidently the eastbound overnight trade was heavier than westbound. The eastbound *Owl* remained nonstop and all Pullman with the *Narragansett* providing the backup with coaches and local stops. Westbound, there was no *Narragansett* backup. Thus, the *Owl* was burdened with coaches and intermediate stops.

Sprinkled into the seventeen weekday trips were the three lightweight speedsters. Overall, there was an emphasis on speed with eight of the thirteen daytime trains concluding their runs in four and a half hours or less. No new speed records were set however. Several of those behemoth Hell Gate Bridge trains even managed to cover the run in just four and a half hours, a new speed record for the Bridge route.

Midland Route Commentary

As a through Boston–New York route, the old White Train route via Willimantic ended service in the 1930s. A pair of regional trains continued to offer service between Boston and Hartford via Willimantic. In 1957, the tracks between Putnam and Willimantic were taken out of service because of earlier flood damage. A few years later the rails were lifted, ending forever the through trains and the route itself.

Utilization of the Hell Gate Bridge

At long last in 1952, the Pennsylvania Railroad began to do something about replacing their deplorable Northeast Corridor equipment. The Pennsy introduced a sleek and completely new *Senator* operating between Boston, New York, and Washington, DC, via Hell Gate Bridge. With its silver sides and observation car, it was very much the equal of the *Merchants Limited.* In addition, the Pennsy provided half of the new equipment needed to completely refurbish the *Colonial* and the *Federal,* while the New Haven Railroad upgraded the *Patriot* with their latest and best equipment. That left just three old clunkers over the Bridge, the *Quaker,* the *William Penn,* and the mail train sometimes called the *Hell Gate Express.* That eighth Hell Gate Bridge frequency, the *Montrealor/ Washingtonian* would be partially reequipped with contributions from several roads.

The Pennsylvania Railroad's efforts were too little and too late. Too little, in that barely 20 percent of its Corridor trains south of New York City were reequipped before the treasury ran dry. Too late to stop dissatisfied business travelers from defecting to the large and relatively roomy DC-6, DC-7, Constellation, and Electra airplanes. As a result, traffic over the Hell Gate Bridge remained frozen at eight trains each way. One of the eight trains, the westbound *Hell Gate Express* ran and carried a rider coach but the train was not advertised.

Off-corridor traffic over the Hell Gate Bridge, which once supported a solid train to Pittsburgh and another to Miami, Florida, had dwindled to one lone through sleeper between Boston and Pittsburgh. Most through travelers would now have to switch trains in Penn Station, New York City.

Ominously, this was also the year the Boston–Florida travelers were offered three-hour rides to Miami via a Boeing 707 aircraft.

10-5 The apogee of the passenger steam engine

Author's collection

An I-5 Shoreline Steam Engine
Courtesy of Allyn Fuller Papers,
Archives & Special Collections at the
Thomas J. Dodd Research Center,
University of Connecticut Libraries

On the left is the New York Central's Niagara, a 4-8-4 Northern, the road's last steam engine. It was introduced in 1945 just as World War II was ending and immediately pressed into Harmon (New York)–Chicago service leading name-brand passenger trains (except the favored few that rated EMD F-7 diesels). On this late winter day of 1949, a Niagara hurries #39, the *North Shore Limited*, through Crugers, New York. Just eleven years after its introduction, the Niagara was retired, bowing to the diesels.

On the right is the New Haven Railroad's Shoreline, a streamlined 4-6-4. It was introduced in 1937, and it was also the last steam engine to be ordered by the New Haven. It performed yeoman's work during World War II in freight and passenger service right alongside the legendary Alco DL 109s. However, when the Alco PAs began arriving in 1948, it was bumped down a notch or two on the Shore Line. Here again, the New Haven's best steam engine finally bowed out in favor of the diesel engine in 1956. Like the Niagara, the Shoreline engine quit when it was still in its prime and closed out the use of steam power on the Shore Line Route.

Market Share in 1957

What a difference ten years make! The near-euphoria of 1947 was replaced with deepening gloom by 1957. Market share had fallen to an estimated 25 percent of through, end-point travelers. It seemed that everybody was picking up share from the railroad. The Connecticut Turnpike attracted more motorists and made interstate bus travel close to time-competitive. New aircraft, including jets, allowed commercial aviation to expand its market share. Business travelers were the first to leave the railroad. To attract and hold leisure travelers, the railroad was forced to keep fares low, which helped the treasury not at all.

Chapter 11: 1957–1969

Dark Days

It was difficult finding much good news in the twelve-year period from 1957 to 1969. The winds of change were blowing and with breathtaking severity. Even if the directors of 1957 knew of the looming competitive changes, their New Haven Railroad simply did not have the capital needed to fortify their position. For example, ending the expensive and time-consuming barge transfer from Bay Ridge to Greenville, New Jersey, with that long-planned three-mile tunnel would have helped. So too would extending electrification from New Haven to Boston. So would freedom to compete with trucks without endless rate hassles with the Interstate Commerce Commission. Scarce capital was needed to upgrade the mainline roadbed and to modernize the once vaunted but now aging electrification system. In brief, the New Haven Railroad was a short-haul carrier with an eroding traffic base and high costs associated with the operation of so many passenger trains. It was capital intensive but was losing its traffic base needed to generate capital.

The word *subsidy* entered here as several state agencies began to offer the troubled road some financial help with their suburban operations.

By the late 1950s, the interstate highway network was stretching its tentacles. Interstate 95 ran virtually parallel to the rail line's Shore Line route. Rival trucks, buses, and cars siphoned off tonnage and travelers.

The competitive attack was not limited to the ground. In 1961, Eastern Airlines introduced Boston–New York (and Boston–Washington, DC) air shuttles. This move revolutionized corridor travel and moved commercial aviation from its somewhat rarified position of a reserved-seat airplane to something akin to the Times Square–Grand Central Shuttle.

Eastern Airlines introduced hourly service starting at 6:00 a.m. and extending through 8:00 p.m. from the end points, initially using Lockheed Constellations and Electras. Travelers to New York could access either Newark or LaGuardia airport. No reservations were necessary, and everyone was guaranteed a seat if they were on hand by the hourly departure time. The airline reportedly would roll out an extra airplane for just one passenger, if necessary. In the few cases where this actually happened, the airline publicity department was on hand to film it.

Business travelers loved the shuttle. Now the carrier was subordinate to the needs of the traveler. No need to wait until 5:00 p.m. for that previously reserved seat on the *Merchants Limited* if the traveler was ready to go at, say, 3:00 p.m. The traveler cabbed it over to the airport, arriving fifteen minutes before the hour. There were few if any security checkpoints back then (hard to believe today). Toting perhaps a bag and a briefcase, our traveler simply marched through the terminal (no security lines, no check-in lines) and right up to the shuttle's gate. Here travelers filled in their name and address on a card, tore off a portion, deposited it in a box, and used the other half of the card as their boarding pass. Free coffee was available at the gate, if desired. Once on board, the traveler took any available seat. Once aloft, two flight attendants rolled the Lazy Susan cart down the aisle for the purpose of selling the traveler a ticket, with credit cards accepted.

Instead of one or two really fast planes, every plane was an express. This move pretty well emptied the Boston–New York overnight trains. The traveler could sleep at home and catch an early flight the following morning, arriving in the business centers of New York or Boston by 9:00 a.m., airport cab time included. By contrast, the railroad could not reach the opposite end point much before noon, thus wasting the entire morning on travel. To schedule a train out of Boston at 5:00 a.m. or 6:00 a.m. was still considered a bit uncivilized.

Cutting Costs

As this ghastly twelve-year period began in 1957, the directors of the New Haven Railroad recognized they would need to start cutting costs with a machete rather than fool any longer with a paring knife and cutesy little lightweight trains. Their first move was to introduce the Electro-Motive FL-9, a locomotive capable of operating as a traditional diesel electric locomotive but capable of changing to a straight electric engine using third rail as a power source in the three-mile Grand Central tunnel approach, thus keeping diesel fumes out of Grand Central Terminal (illustration 11-1). There would be no need to change engines in New Haven. In fact, with enough FL-9s, there would be scant need for overhead wire except for the Woodlawn Junction–Stamford section because of the suburban multiple-unit electrics. The entire Bay Ridge freight line could be dewired with diesels operating straight through. Hell Gate Bridge passenger trains could operate with diesels as far as Sunnyside, New York. The Van Nest electric shops could be closed, with only multiple-unit suburban trains still operating under wire from Grand Central to Stamford. The entire twenty-one-mile Danbury Branch could be and was dewired in 1962. The enormous advantages of electric power, first introduced in 1907, were now considered relics and a liability. Fortunately not all of this downgrading came to pass, and the main line to New Haven was spared.

11-1 The New Haven Railroad's unique FL-9 locomotive
Courtesy of New Haven Railroad Historical & Technical Association Inc. Collection

The New Haven Railroad's unique EMD FL-9 locomotives could operate as diesels or as third-rail electrics. These units are seen at Boston's Dover Street Yards sometime during the 1960s. This photo appeared in the photo feature "South Bay Jct. and Dover Street Yards Revisited," *Shoreliner*. Volume 22, Issue 1, 1991. Bill Wheeler photo. A detailed history of the New Haven's FL-9 electric-diesel-electrics, titled "New Haven's Unique FL-9," can be found in *Shoreliner* Volume 25, Issues 2 through 4, 1994.

The Niagara passenger train engine

11-2 Niagara engine at Harmon, New York
Author's collection

Here we see the mighty Niagara engine, barely ten years old and running off its final miles in mid–1950s. In this scene, it is departing Harmon, demoted to pulling a semiexpress train to Syracuse. No more assignments like pulling the *Advanced Commodore Vanderbilt* or the *Wolverine* as far as Buffalo. Rather, this ultimate steam machine is relegated to serving commuters bound for stops on the Upper Hudson Line or west from Albany to the host of smaller towns that dotted the Mohawk River.

11-3 Niagara engine moving through Crugers, New York
Author's collection

A Niagara is getting #367, the Upstate Special, up to speeds as it breezes through Crugers. Note the telegraph poles still carry some active wire. Alas, the Niagara was never allowed to operate on the Boston and Albany because of its size and weight.

11-4 An Alco PA smokes it up leaving Harmon in 1948
Author's collection

An Alco PA, true to form, smokes it up as it attempts a rapid acceleration out of Harmon with #15, the *Ohio State Limited.* It was carded to cover the New York to Buffalo run at a blistering seven hours and twenty-six minutes, the Central's fastest scheduled train between these two points (in the 1940s).

11-5 Fairbanks–Morse Consolidated Line locomotive in 1950
Author's collection

Fairbanks–Morse Consolidated Line has an A and a B unit, packing four thousand horsepower and hurrying this freight train over the Inland Route in 1950. It is, of course, properly attired in the New York Central's *Lightning Stripes*. The Boston and Albany was tread by virtually every locomotive type, except for the 4-8-4 Niagara's. Yes, that huge slab of steel on the locomotive's cowcatcher could be parted, if necessary, to reveal a coupler.

Bankruptcy Again

The 1961 introduction of the Eastern Airline's Shuttle was the straw that broke the camel's back. With freight and passenger revenues plummeting (and a recession to boot), the New Haven Railroad, just fourteen years out of its first bankruptcy, entered it again. From this bankruptcy, the trustees concluded there could be no viable reorganization. The entire railroad was imploding, a pathetic vestige of the "gilt-edged" railroad of fifty years earlier.

Were this railroad not so strategically placed in the Northeast Corridor, outright abandonment might have occurred. Still, its purely regional and suburban traffic as an alternative to highways was considered essential. Enough state and federal subsidy was forthcoming to keep the patient alive, if not well.

The once-mighty New York Central System and the Pennsylvania Railroad merged in February 1968 to form the Penn Central Railroad. As a condition to approving this merger of parallel lines, the federal regulators of the time were quite ready to assume government ownership of subways and local transit systems but certainly not an entire railroad! Rather, they made their approval of the Penn Central merger conditioned on the willingness of the newly merged firm to take in the New Haven Railroad as a part of their family. This happened in January 1969. At the end of 1968, the New Haven Railroad ceased to be, ending ninety-six years of continuous operation under this name (illustrations 11-6 through 11-14). This unwanted orphan in 1968 was essentially a giant passenger railroad operating longer-distance as well as regional and purely suburban trains. Only a handful of freight trains remained. By forcing the erstwhile wealthy New York Central and Pennsylvania railroads to adopt this orphan, all would be well, and the issue of public ownership or subsidy could be avoided. This was the flawed logic of the Interstate Commerce Commission in 1969.

11-6 The last public timetable published by the New Haven Railroad

The New Haven Railroad published its first public timetable in 1872. Unfortunately, we have yet to discover a copy of this first document. However, we can present the very last full-service public timetable, published ninety-six years later in 1968. All the illustrations from 11-6 through 11-14 are from the 1986 New Haven Railroad's public timetable.

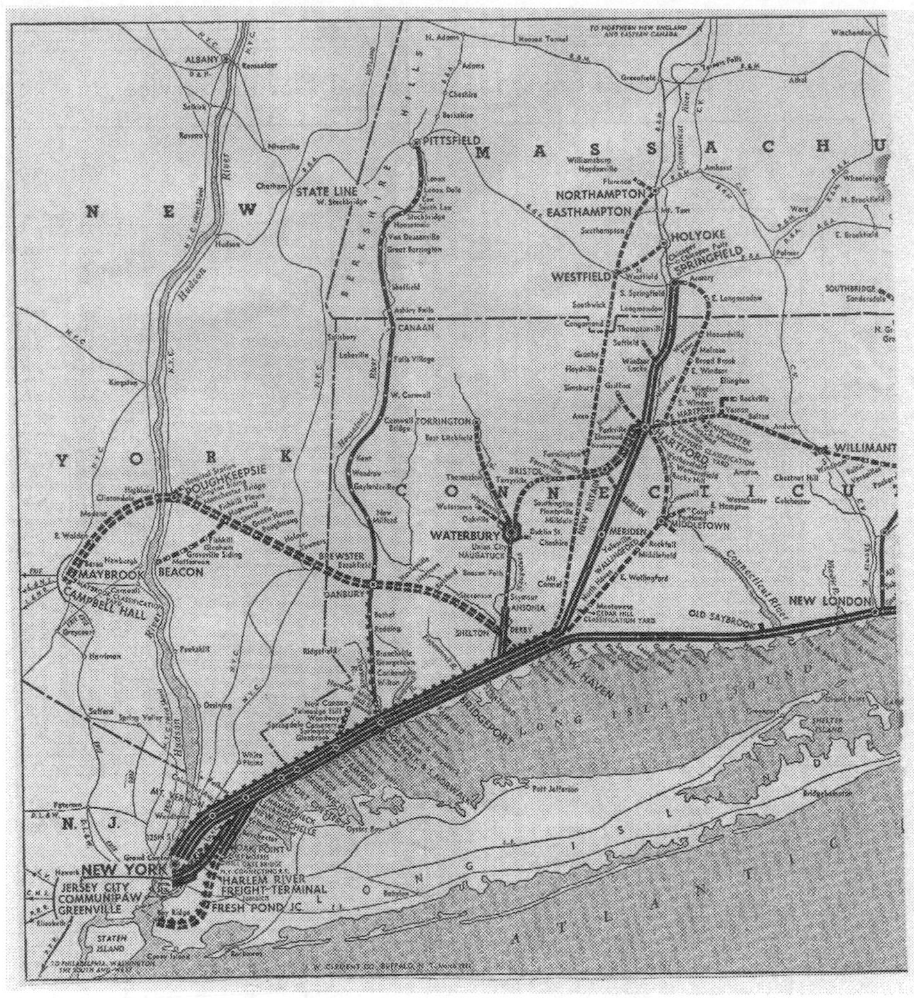

11-7 The New Haven Railroad route system at its demise (1968)
Public Timetable

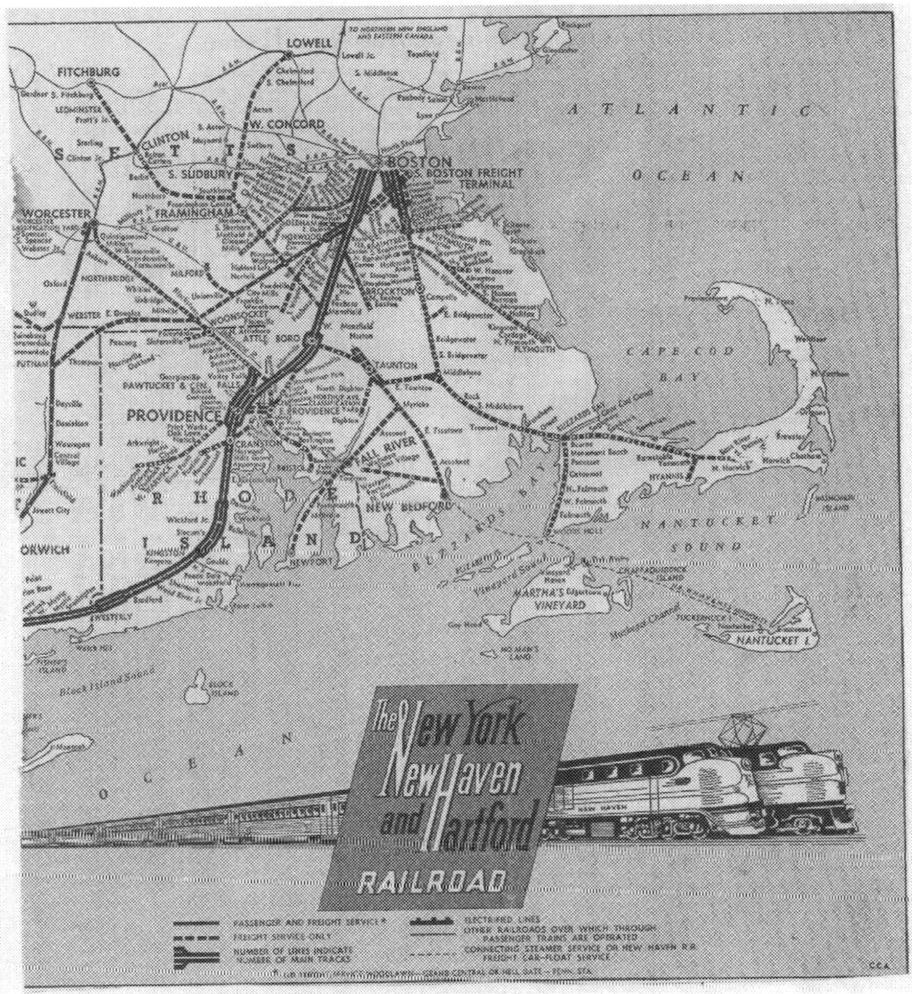

11-7 The New Haven Railroad route system at its demise (1968) Public Timetable

Here is what the New York, New Haven and Hartford Railroad looked like in 1968 just before the end. Compare this with a similar map of their operated lines in 1910, (illustrations 11-8a and b) when the railroad was built out to its maximum extent.

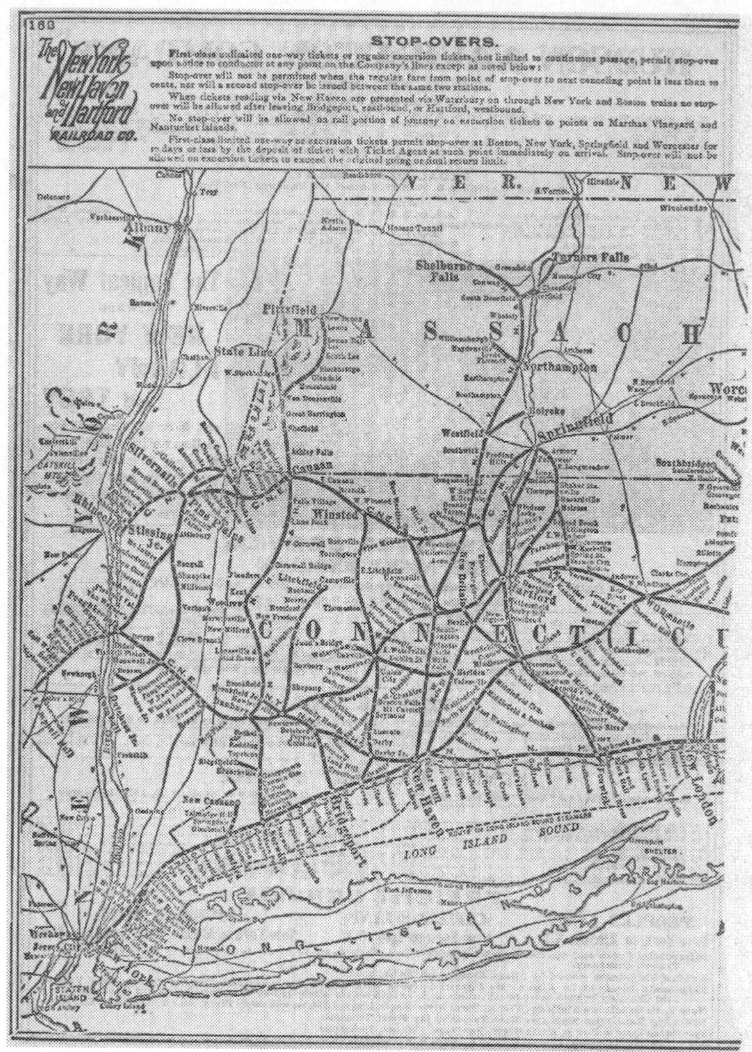

11-8 The New Haven Railroad route system at its peak (1910) Public Timetable

This 1910 map of the railroad was precisely when the New Haven Railroad also owned virtually every trolley company and every steamship company in Southern New England—a tight little monopoly led by banker J. P. Morgan and his faithful servant and New Haven president, Charles S. Mellen, from 1903 to 1913.

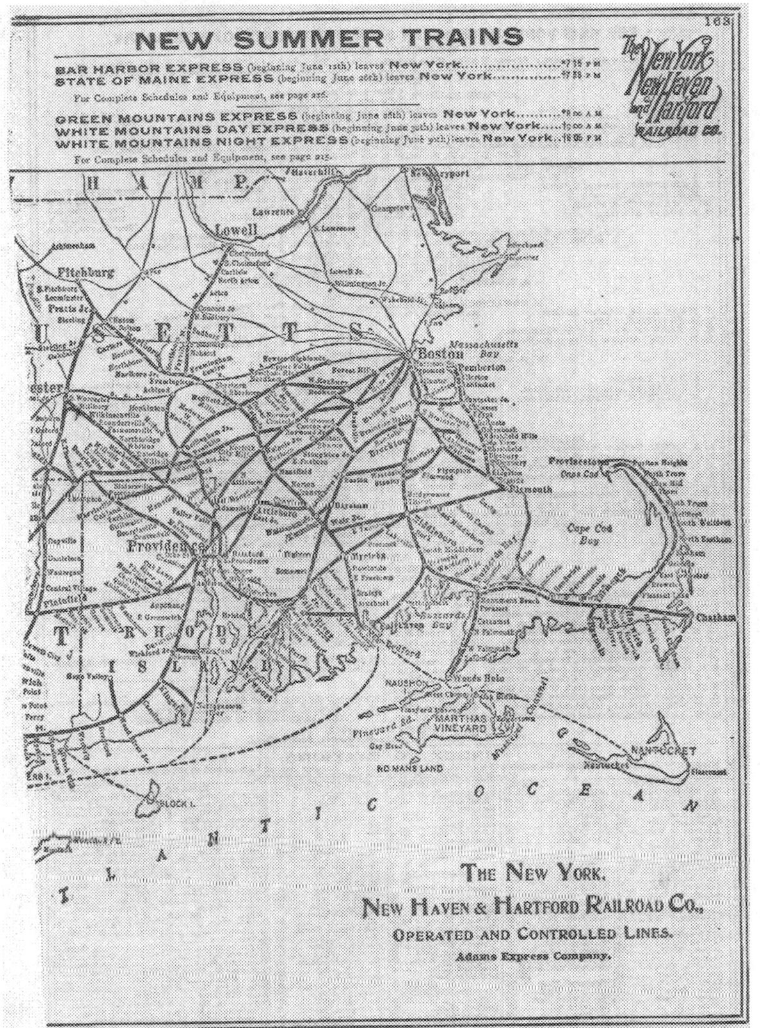

11-8 The New Haven Railroad route system at its peak
(1910)
Public Timetable

The New Haven Railroad was at its prime issuing "widows and orphans" stock whose shares were indeed "gilt-edged." However, by the 1968 going-out-of-business sale, much of this property was either worthless or had already been abandoned. Why this great fall?

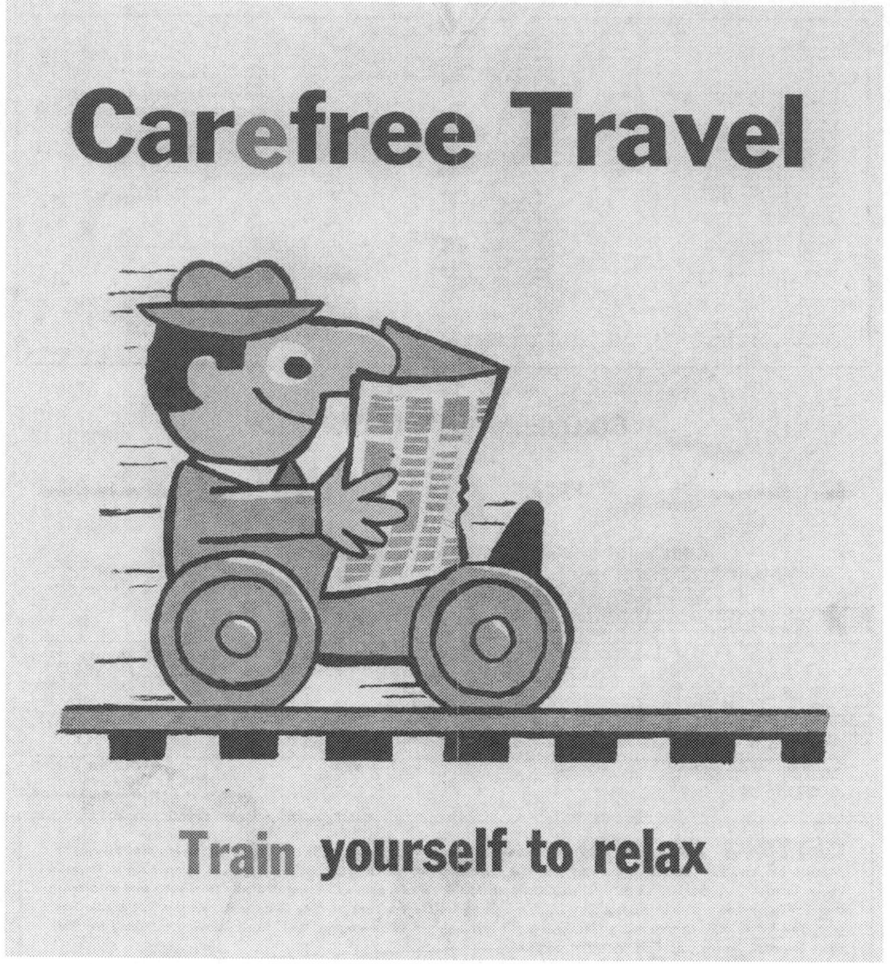

11-9 Train yourself to relax
Public timetable

Would the busy, overworked business executive abandon the plane or his car and *train* himself to relax instead?

Like to feel regal? We have just the palace for you!

A Venetian one (presently termed Gardner Museum) in Boston's Fenway. Completed in 1903, it was first named Mrs. Jack Gardner's Palace. This illustrious lady founded and created a world apart. Weathered statuary of Old World look (some of it from Renaissance villas, some from Italian gardens before the fall of Rome); flowers of breathtaking beauty and fragrance tended by a staff of six gardeners; a private chapel and a music room all blend in so richly with marvelous works of art collected in competition with the great museums of Europe. Plan your palace visit soon—we'll get you on your way so you too may experience and enjoy this touch of past splendor.

Interested in "INNER SPACE"?

We make it available every day. And we'd like to offer it to you when your thoughts approach the travel stage. "Innerspace" is easy to come by on The Train —a stroll to the Smoking Lounge Section to enjoy a smoke . . . a friendly chat with a fellow traveler—on to The Diner or Grill Car for more enjoyment—an apéritif . . . a delicious Luncheon or Dinner (sample a real New England dish — they're great) — now to rest your "inner self" with a stroll back to your coach seat or Parlor Car Chair (incidentally, just $2.37 more than your regular coach fare on the New Haven R.R.) for a bit of a nap . . . a return to the best seller you brought along . . . or a session of vista viewing through the train window. Soon you'll hear the announcement: "Back Bay Station next" or perhaps "Grand Central—last stop", or wherever your destination may be. Your trip was really short in time but long in pleasure wasn't it?

DOES YOUR GROUP GROPE AROUND?

at times for club programs that are different, that build up interest, attendance and new memberships? We suspect so (every group seems to be faced with such problems). Why not consider a Group Travel Train Trip? Say to New York, Boston, Mystic Seaport and other interesting places? You'll travel together and enjoy together the theatre, opera, sports events and lots else. And you'll save money with our special reduced fares for ten or more of your club group. Our ticket agents will gladly assist you or your program chairman with the details. We'd like to welcome your group aboard The New Haven soon. Can we plan on it?

11-10 Take the train and enjoy!
Public timetable

Here's the pitch to a more leisurely crowd. Wouldn't the promise of more "inner space" strike a responsive chord with today's air traveler? Skip the smoking reference, of course.

4 **Fares** (Subject to Change)

BOSTON, MASS. TO	RAILROAD FARES — In Coaches — One Way	In Coaches — * 2 Day Round Trip	In Coaches — 30 Day Round Trip	In A Parlor Cars — One Way	In A Parlor Cars — 30 Day Round Trip	In Sleeping Cars or Parlor Cars — One Way	In Sleeping Cars or Parlor Cars — 30 Day Round Trip	Parlor Car — Seat Note A	SLEEPING CAR FARES — Lower Berth	Upper Berth	Roomette — One Person	Bedroom — One Person	Bedroom — Two or more Persons	Bedroom Suite
Altoona, Pa.	27.92	.....	51.91	36.96	70.89	40.78	77.74	.....	g 6.71	g 5.06	g 11.22	g 19.90	g 19.90	g 36.10
Baltimore, Md.	21.23	.....	40.18	26.44	50.37	30.25	57.42	4.57	6.71	5.06	11.22	16.25	19.90	32.45
Bridgeport, Conn.	8.80	9.36	15.66	8.80	15.89	11.87	21.06	2.37	5.39	4.07	8.47	11.25	13.95	22.50
Harrisburg, Pa.	21.71	.....	41.11	27.00	51.63	30.28	58.68	.....	g 6.71	g 5.06	g 11.22	g 19.90	g 19.90	g 36.10
Jacksonville, Fla.	♦49.00	.....	♦93.75	.....	.....	♦70.70	♦133.09	.....	15.45	11.90	21.75	38.05	38.05	68.85
Kingston, R. I.	3.71	4.26	6.70	3.71	6.70			2.37						
Miami, Fla.	♦61.25	.....	♦115.75	.....	.....	♦87.82	♦165.69	.....	19.80	15.00	27.55	45.40	48.40	83.95
Newark, N. J.	13.00	.....	23.70	19.72	25.13	17.58	31.96	3.90	6.21	5.06	11.22	16.25	19.90	32.45
New Haven, Conn.	7.96	8.53	14.40	7.96	14.40	10.58	19.05	2.37	5.39	4.07	8.47	11.25	13.95	22.50
New London, Conn.	5.45	6.00	9.85	5.45	9.85			2.37						
New York, N. Y.	11.58	12.13	20.85	11.58	20.85	15.36	27.70	2.37	5.39	4.07	8.47	11.25	13.95	22.50
Philadelphia, Pa.	18.78	.....	31.28	19.23	38.13	23.33	42.98	3.52	6.21	5.06	11.22	16.25	19.90	32.45
Pittsburgh, Pa.	32.43	.....	57.70	44.63	84.80	48.43	91.45	.....	g 6.71	g 5.06	g 11.22	g 19.90	g 19.90	g 36.10
Providence, R. I.	2.37	2.82	4.30	2.37	4.30			2.37						
Route 128, Mass.	.85	.....	1.60	.93	1.80			2.37						
St. Petersburg, Fla.	♦57.43	.....	♦108.90	.....	.....	♦82.47	♦156.28	.....	18.60	14.35	26.00	43.00	43.00	78.35
Stamford, Conn.	9.92	10.47	17.90	9.92	17.93	13.17	23.75	2.37	5.39	4.07	8.47	11.25	13.95	22.50
Trenton, N. J.	15.22	.....	30.13	17.00	31.69	20.81	38.54	3.03	6.71	5.06	11.22	16.25	19.90	32.45
Washington, D. C.	23.13	.....	43.98	29.30	56.29	33.11	63.14	5.12	6.71	5.06	11.22	16.25	19.90	32.45
Westerly, R. I.	4.94	5.09	8.20	4.94	8.23			2.37						
West Palm Beach, Fla.	♦59.08	.....	♦111.75	.....	.....	♦84.71	♦160.29	.....	19.20	14.70	27.15	44.65	44.65	82.50
Wilmington, Del.	17.69	.....	33.47	21.17	40.03	24.98	46.89	3.60	6.71	5.06	11.22	16.25	19.90	32.45

SO-You're landlocked

Well, if you wish, we'll carry you away by train to an island. An island bounded by the Harlem River, East River, North River and the Hudson River. It's Manhattan Island, just chock full of pleasures for everybody—by day, by night, by early morn, no matter the season. AND we'll get your pleasure-filled self back to your landlocked existence (if you want to return). You see we have round trip fares and round trip service.

SEEING is BELIEVING

Perhaps you've heard or seen our constant reference to The Scenic Shore Line Route BUT have you ever traveled it between New York and Boston (on right hand side from New York, left hand side from Boston)? If not, we'd like to welcome you aboard soon to see for yourself what all our message-sending is about. You'll know then what we mean! We have an idea you'll be one of our regulars thereafter.

11-11 Sightseeing and low train fares in 1968
Public Timetable

Just take a glance at those 1968 train fares. Boston to New York, one way was $11.58. A two-day round trip was $12.13, and a thirty-day round trip was $20.85. Add $2.37 to upgrade any segment to a first-class parlor-car seat! Talk about a fire-sale pricing!

Of course the "Let's Face It Fellows" ad unmasks the old boy club of chauvinists, each of whom presumably kept a "little woman" who just adored him?? If space is in short supply, here's where we can recover some of it.

Shore Line 5

BOSTON AND PROVIDENCE TO NEW YORK AND PHILADELPHIA—WASHINGTON

Consult Penn. Central local time tables for complete schedules between New York and Washington.

	THE OWL			The Hell Gate	The Mayflower	The Colonial	The Mayflower	The Mayflower	The Senator	The 42nd Street	The Patriot	The Puritan	The Gilt Edge		MERCHANTS LIMITED	The Sundown	The Pershing Square
	Daily	Daily	Mon thru Fri Ex Hol A	Mon thru Sat Ex Hol A	Sun & Hol A only	Daily	Sat only	Mon thru Fri Ex Hol A	Daily	Daily	Daily	Daily	Daily	Mon thru Fri Ex Hol A	Daily	Daily	Sun & Hol D only
	3	189 PC ♦135	♦401-♦67	181 PC 171	17	♦171	19	9	♦173	♦13	♦175	15	♦39	♦521	♦27	♦33	43
	AM	AM	AM	AM	AM	AM	AM	AM	AM	AM	PM	PM	PM	PM	PM	PM	PM
Boston, Mass. South Station ... Lv	2 00	......	......	6 45	7 30	8 00	8 30	9 00	10 00	11 00	1 00	2 30	4 00	......	5 00	6 00	7 00
Back Bay	2 05	......	......	6 50	7 35	8 05	8 35	9 05	10 05	11 05	1 05	2 35	4 05	......	5 05	6 05	7 05
Route 128, Mass. ♦	2 26	......	......	7 02	7 49	8 18	8 48	9 18	10 21	11 16	1 19	2 51	4 19	......	gg	6 18	7 19
Providence, R. I. ... Lv	3 20	......	......	8 00	8 25	8 54	9 24	9 54	10 56	11 55	1 56	3 30	4 54	5 18	5 55	6 54	7 58
Kingston, R. I.	......	......	......	8 27	8 51	......	9 50	......	11 22	......	......	3 58	5 30	5 47	dd	7 21	8 22
Westerly, R. I.	......	......	......	8 43	9 09	......	10 09	......	......	12 35	......	4 17	5 35	6 07	......	7 39	8 41
New London, Conn.	4 38	......	6 36	9 14	9 31	9 54	10 30	10 54	11 59	12 58	2 56	4 41	6 00	6 31	6 54	8 02	9 05
Old Saybrook, Conn.	......	......	6 48	9 36	9 52	......	10 51	......	12 20	......	3 16	5 02	6 23	......	......	8 23	9 27
New Haven, Conn. ... Due	5 34	......	7 40	10 10	10 25	10 45	11 25	11 43	12 54	1 50	3 50	5 38	6 57	......	7 46	8 58	10 07
New Haven, Conn. ... Lv	5 53	6 35	8g32	10 25	10a34	10 54	11a32	11a57	1 03	2s08	3 58	5 45	7 05	......	7 53	9 07	10 15
Bridgeport, Conn. ... Due	6 18	6 56	......	10 46	......	11 14	......	......	1 23	......	4 19	6 05	7 26	......	......	9 28	10 35
Norwalk and South Norwalk, Conn.	mm	......	......	......	......	......	......	......	......	......	......	......	7 44	......	......	......	......
Stamford, Conn.	6 44	cc	......	11 13	......	11 36	......	......	1 50	......	kk	......	7 58	......	......	9 53	11 01
New York 125th Street ☒ ♦	7 20	......	......	......	11s47	......	12s46	1s09	......	3s15	......	7 05	8 34	......	9 05	10 30	11 37
New York Grand Central Term. ... Due	7 33	......	9g27	......	11s55	......	12s55	1s20	......	3s28	......	7 15	8 45	......	9 15	10 40	11 45
New York Pennsylvania Station ... Due	......	8 10	......	12 00	......	12 25	......	......	2 40	......	5 35	......	......	......	......	......	......
Penn. Central: Newark, N. J.	......	9h46	......	a1h01	......	1s01	......	......	3 16	......	6 01	......	......	......	......	......	......
Trenton, N. J.	......	10h29	......	a1h46	......	1s46	......	......	4 00	......	aa	......	......	......	......	......	......
North Philadelphia, Pa.	......	10h56	......	a2h13	......	2s13	......	......	4 29	......	7 15	......	......	......	......	......	......
Philadelphia, Pa. (30th Street Station)	......	11h05	......	2h22	......	2 22	......	......	4 39	......	7 24	......	......	......	......	......	......
Wilmington, Del.	......	11h37	......	a2h53	......	2s53	......	......	5 08	......	7 52	......	......	......	......	......	......
Baltimore, Md. (Pennsylvania Station)	......	12h38	......	a3h58	......	3s58	......	......	6 09	......	8 53	......	......	......	......	......	......
Washington, D. C. ... Due	......	1h20	......	4h40	......	4 40	......	......	6 50	......	9 36	......	......	......	......	......	......
	AM	PM	AM	PM	AM	PM	PM	PM	PM	PM	PM	PM	PM	PM	PM	PM	PM

	The Pilgrim	The Pilgrim	The Pilgrim	THE FEDERAL	The New Yorker	The New Yorker	The New Yorker	THE OWL	
	Sun only	Sat only	Mon thru Fri	Sun thru Fri Nights Note 1	Sun Nights only	Mon thru Fri Nights	Sat Nights only	Daily	
	199	197	♦179	177	189 PC ♦131	187 PC ♦131	187 PC ♦111	3	
	PM	PM	PM	PM	PM	PM	PM	AM	
Boston, Mass. South Station Lv	9 00	9 00	9 00	10 10	11 45	11 45	11 45	2 00	......
Back Bay	9 05	9 05	9 10	10 15	11 50	11 50	11 50	2 05	......
Route 128, Mass. ♦	9 20	9 22	9 30	10 30	12 05	12 07	12 07	2 26	......
Providence, R. I. ... Lv	10 04	10 28	10 45	11 10	1 06	1 25	1 26	3 20	......
Kingston, R. I.	10 31	10 53	11 12	......	......	......	......	......	......
Westerly, R. I.	10 50	11 13	11 30	......	......	......	......	......	......
New London, Conn.	11 14	11d47	11 58	12 10	2 13	2 37	2 37	4 38	......
Old Saybrook, Conn.	11 38	12 08	12 20	......	......	......	......	......	......
New Haven, Conn. ... Due	12 14	12 45	12 58	1 04	3 08	3 33	3 33	5 34	......
New Haven, Conn. ... Lv	12 26	1 03	1 20	1 27	3 23	4 06	4 08	5 53	......
Bridgeport, Conn. ... Due	12 44	1 20	1 37	......	3 46	4 26	4 25	6 16	......
Norwalk and South Norwalk, Conn.	1 04	1 43	2 04	......	......	......	......	mm	......
Stamford, Conn.	1 18	1 57	2 18	......	4 15	4 56	4 36	6 44	......
New York 125th Street ☒ ♦	......	......	......	......	......	......	......	7 20	......
New York Grand Cen. Ter. Due	......	......	......	......	......	......	......	7 33	......
New York Penna. Station ... Due	2 10	3 00	3 38	2 55	5 30	5 55	5 55	......	......
Penn. Central: Newark, N. J.	......	......	......	[illegible]	6e45	6e45	8e16	......	......
Trenton, N. J.	......	......	......	[illegible]	[illegible]	7e32	[illegible]	......	......
North Philadelphia, Pa.	......	......	......	4e57	8e00	8e00	9e35	......	......
Philadelphia, Pa. (30th St. Station)	......	......	......	5e05	8e10	8e10	9e35	......	......
Wilmington, Del.	......	......	......	5e46	8e38	8e38	10e08	......	......
Baltimore (Pennsylvania Station)	......	......	......	[illegible]	[illegible]	[illegible]	11e00	......	......
Washington, D. C. ... Due	......	......	......	7 45	10e20	10e30	11e50	......	......
	AM	AM	AM	AM	AM	AM	AM	AM	

☒ Stops of inbound trains at 125th Street Station, New York, are only to leave passengers.
♦ No baggage handled; when reference appears against station, check baggage to nearest station having facilities.
Holidays A—May 30, July 4, Sept. 2, Nov. 28, Dec. 25, 1968 and Jan. 1, 1969.
Holidays D—Sept. 2, Dec. 25, 1968 and Jan. 1, 1969.
Holidays I—May 30, July 4 and Sept. 2, 1968.
Note 1—On nights of Dec. 24 and 31 only, 1968. Sleeping Cars handled from New York to Washington in PC No. 111, leaving New York 8.00 AM, due Washington 11.30 AM, coach passenger change at New York to PC No. 111.
a No checked baggage service provided at this station for this train.
c Change trains at New York. No connection on May 30, July 4 and Sept. 2.
d Due New London 11.38 PM.
e Coach passengers change trains at New York.
g Change trains at New Haven.
h Change trains at New York.
aa Stops only on Saturdays, Sundays and Holidays I at Trenton, N. J. at 6.48 PM.
cc Stops only on Sundays and Holidays A at Stamford, Conn. at 7.20 AM.
dd Stops only to receive passengers at Kingston Sundays only June 30 to Sept. 8, Incl., 1968, also Sept. 2, 1968 at 6.19 PM.
gg Stops only to take passengers at Route 128, 5.20 PM.
kk Stops only on Sundays and Holiday A at Stamford 4.42 PM.
mm Stops only on Sundays and Holidays A at Norwalk and South Norwalk at 6.33 AM.
(220-219) 5-12-68—9

11-12 The diner or the grill car for delicious meals
Public Timetable

There is some nostalgia when considering how easy and convenient it once was to stroll down to the diner or grill car and enjoy the freshly made chowder, the broiled fish, or the New England boiled dinner, topped off with a cup of fresh coffee and a plate of Indian pudding (maybe with a scoop of vanilla ice cream?) for dessert. This kind of style is totally lacking in today's coach travel, and but a thin reminder of what had once been universal in first class.

MIDTOWN
DOWNTOWN
UPTOWN
EASTSIDE
WESTSIDE
ALL AROUND THE TOWN

NEW YORK

Welcomes Your Visits

AND The New Haven's Ticket Agents welcome your visits also—to arrange for your New York WEEKENDS in The Big Town. These weekends are scheduled once a month on specific dates from Boston, Route 128 and Providence, New London, New Haven, Springfield and Hartford. Besides your Round Trip Coach Ticket you get Hotel Accommodations and Hotel Breakfast each morning. You'll arrive relaxed on The Train right in midtown Manhattan—just the right way to get started right on your weekend whirl around town. Picture yourself (and your family or perhaps your club group) atop Empire State Building, visiting some monarchs of the Seven Seas, shopping The Avenue (Fifth, of course), doing Radio City, cruising aboard the Staten Island Ferry, wending your way about Chinatown. Enough hints for now! You get the picture don't you! There's only one drawback—we wish we could accompany you as there's a lot we haven't discovered about magical Manhattan ourselves. So go on ahead—have yourself a ball—you will!

BOSTON BYWAYS ARE FOR BROWSING!

Bookshops
Antique Shops
Museums
The Public Garden
Art Galleries
The Waterfront
and
lots more besides
you'll discover yourself

$2.92
BUYS YOUR 2 DAY ROUND TRIP TICKET
from
PROVIDENCE

Start Browsing Boston
You'll like it!

LET'S TELL YOU ABOUT OUR SPECIAL COMFORT ITEM!

It's one of the top travel offerings in our stock. It's a Parlor Car Chair. It's a big, soft upholstered chair . . . that reclines, that swivels—that relaxes you. And it's not equipped with a seat belt. You may enjoy its comfort anywhere on The New Haven. The Price Tag $2.37 represents just the amount collectible when you hold a regular fare one way coach ticket. Round trip 30 Day Coach tickets and Family Travel Plan tickets are also acceptable in the transaction. Oh—there's a Parlor Car Attendant in the car also—he specializes in quiet service that so many folks like—you will too. This is a year 'round item—in stock every day. Let's reserve one for you—may we? It's a bargain too good to miss!

TRAIN YOURSELF TO RELAX

(200) 5-12-68—7

11-13 Visiting, browsing, and a special comfort item!
Public timetable

In case you are still not convinced of the fun times ahead of you (especially if you properly *train* yourself), try these specials dealing with sightseeing, browning, and deep-down comfort.

STRICTLY CONFIDENTIAL

is the manner in which the New Haven's Industrial Development Department staff will handle your inquiries. We are at your service to assist you in the selection of the best site for your new industry. Does your growing business necessitate expansion and relocation? You'll find help in that direction too. Up-to-the minute data records are accessible for your examination. Aid in the aspect of community planning is another valuable service rendered. New York and Southern New England has much to offer industry; abundant water supply, power a'plenty, productive working force and a moderate climate in addition to many other benefits. Yes, this region is a good place to settle in. Think it over. We would like very much to arrange a conference with your people to fill them in with the facts and figures for their consideration. You'll find such a meeting will bring fruitful results. There's nothing we would like more than to have the pleasure of your company in New Haven Territory. Just indicate your interest—we'll work things out for you—in strictest confidence of course!

Mr. E. J. Barrett, General Manager
INDUSTRIAL DEVELOPMENT DEPT.
The New Haven R.R.
South Station, Boston, Mass. 02210
292 Madison Ave., New York, N.Y. 10017

11-14 Grow your business here—strictly confidential
Public Timetable

Can you imagine a more lonely and thankless job than working in the Industrial Development Department of the soon-to-be-defunct New Haven Railroad?

The successor company, Conrail, did keep some freight trackage of its former New Haven Road. Within ten years, Conrail had managed to divest itself of most of the old New Haven property. The Shore Line and the Springfield Line went to Amrak. Metro-North bought fifty-six miles of the former Shore Line Route, affording Amtrak trackage rights over it. Several short-line railroads bought pieces of the old line so that the Providence and Worcester Railroad would reach out from its original forty-three-mile route.

As a through freight route from southern New England to and through New York City and Southern New York state, the former New Haven line lost both of its western connections. Bay Ridge yard closed in 1974, as did Maybrook (Campbell Hall) when a fire made the Poughkeepsie Bridge inoperable without major repairs, which were not forthcoming. The bridge is now billed as the world's longest bridge over a waterway and reserved just for hikers and bikers. Bay Ridge still has a small vestige of its former status as a major freight-car ferry across the New York Harbor.

The 1969 Weekday Schedules

Some ten months into this forced merger, it was clear the Penn Central Railroad had no plans to revive the Shore Line or any other Boston–New York rail route. Further cutting of service was the goal. The following schedules are from November 1969.

New York		Boston	Boston		New York
7:30 am	The Bostonian	12:05 pm	7:00 am	The New Yorker	11:35 am
9:30 am	The Bay State	1:55 pm	*7:55 am	The Colonial	12:25 pm
*11:15 am	The Colonial	3:50 pm	*9:55 am	The Senator	2:40 pm
12:30 pm	Yankee Clipper	4:50 pm	*12:55 pm	The Patriot	5:25 pm
*2:10 pm	The Senator	6:55 pm	3:00 pm	The Manhattan	7:30 pm
5:00 pm	Merchants Ltd.	9:16 pm	5:00 pm	Merchants Ltd.	9:15 pm
*6:00 pm	The Patriot	10:50 pm	6:00 pm	The Murray Hill	11:00 pm
*3:15 am	The Federal	8:25 am	*10:15 pm	The Federal	2:55 am

Commentary on the Shore Line Route

With just eight weekday departures each way, service frequencies had sunk back to the level of about 1880. But unlike 1880, when further growth was evident, the 1969 schedules were clear indicators that Penn Central was preparing to exit the passenger train business.

One night train survived, the *Federal.* In addition to its Boston–Washington sleepers, it carried a set-out sleeper for New York, which was about all that was left of the *Owl* and the *Narragansett* together.

The three daytime Boston–Washington fliers were spared—the *Colonial,* the *Senator,* and the *Patriot.* The *Merchants Limited,* now a thin shadow of its former self, soldiered on in its tattered uniform, as did the few remaining Boston–Grand Central trains. The proud *Yankee Clipper* eastbound stayed close to its original time slot, but its westbound counterpart disappeared.

Since the railway lost its Railway Post Office cars and contract with the US Postal Service in 1967, there was less head-end work and fewer cars and head-end delays. Still, with deferred maintenance, the roadbed could not support any new speed records with traditional equipment. The *Merchants Limited* with its four-and-a-half-hour end-point times led in speed, equaling only what it had achieved in 1937, thirty-two years prior.

Commentary on the Inland Route

As a through route with solid trains, the Inland Route died in 1952. Still, the 1969 Penn Central offered one Boston–Springfield rail diesel car with a New York connection at Springfield and two daily trips between Worcester and New London with connections at New London for New York. The Worcester–New London trip of seventy-two miles required an additional fifteen minutes over 1957 account of poor track conditions. The Worcester–New York rail traveler still had three departure choices from Worcester—all by rail diesel car and with a necessary change en route.

The Utilization of the Hell Gate Bridge

The great bridge saw its passenger traffic cut in half. Instead of eight daily trains each way, by 1969 there were just four, all Boston–Washington trains. The Montrealor/Washingtonian disappeared into history. Three or four daily freight trains each way still plied the bridge, a considerable frequency decrease because of the inroads of trucks and the beginning of the Penn Central diversion of Bay Ridge traffic to Selkirk and the West Shore Route.

A massive four-track bridge carrying just seven or eight trains each way was far more track capacity than needed. Soon one freight track was removed. The remaining freight track wire was de-energized (but the wire was not removed) in 1959 as diesels bumped the electrics. However, electric freight engines were restored to Bay Ridge in 1962.

Market Share in 1969

How the once-mighty had fallen! A total of 5 percent of all through Boston–New York travelers opted to use rail. This was almost to the point of making rail irrelevant. What was happening in the Boston–New York corridor was happening throughout the country. Save for a few urban or suburban corridors, did our country need passenger trains any longer? Could we not do just fine with a fly-drive and bus transport network? The growth and mass popularization of commercial aviation and the completion of the interstate highway system capitalized in part by government subsidy made the railroad appear like a relic.

This nadir for Boston–New York rail travel began the debate over whether to subsidize a national railroad passenger system. Without such subsidy, the intercity passenger train's demise was near. In the Northeast, the question about needing passenger trains soon extended to freight railroads too. The Penn Central Railroad collapsed into bankruptcy in June 1970 and virtually all other northeast railroads soon followed. Maybe we were about to see the end of the flanged steel wheel on steel rail—passenger and freight. Could trucks, cars, planes, and buses pick up the slack? Congress and government officials so anxious to avoid this scenario could duck the issue no longer.

Chapter 12: 1969–1994

The Earlier Amtrak Years

The Turbotrain's April 1969 introduction in Boston–New York City service was about the only bright spot in an otherwise drab, dreary quarter of a century, 1969 to 1994. The US Department of Transportation ordered two sets of these trains, which allowed for two Boston–New York round trips (illustration 12-1). The schedule was an ambitious three hours and thirty-nine minutes between Grand Central Terminal and Back Bay Station, Boston. For reasons unknown, the Turbotrain terminated in Back Bay instead of completing the run to South Station. Still, the end-point times were a lofty sixty-three-miles-per-hour average speed, raising the bar from the *Merchant Limited's* old record of fifty-seven miles per hour. The Turbos remained in service for seven years until they were withdrawn in 1976.

"A sleek, new lightweight passenger train, the Turbo-Train, enters service in 1968 in the United States and Canada. The TurboTrain is lighter, faster, quieter, smoother and more reliable than conventional trains—and cheaper to run. The TurboTrain, conceived on aerodynamic principles, and powered by aircraft-type gas turbine engines, was designed by United Aircraft Corp-oration. It is being developed and marketed by Surface Transportation Systems, Sikorsky Aircraft Division." Courtesy of Igor I. Sikorsky Historical Archives Inc.

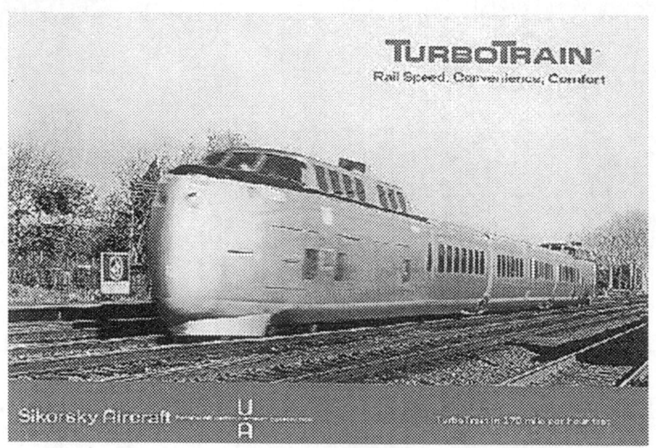

12-1 TurboTrain

Artist's conception of interior
Courtesy of Igor I. Sikorsky
Historical Archives Inc.

Canadian TurboTrain
Courtesy of Igor I. Sikorsky
Historical Archives Inc.

The TurboTrain did better than those three lightweight trains of the 1950s. It established a new end-point speed record, and it remained in service for a total of seven years. Only two of these train sets were built for the New Haven Railroad in 1967 to 1968. With the demise of the New Haven Railroad, Amtrak took over their operation in 1971. No additional sets were ever ordered by Amtrak.

Amtrak TurboTrain
Courtesy of Igor I. Sikorsky Historical Archives Inc.

Why did the public willingly accept the Metroliners, those souped-up multiple-unit electrics on the New York–Washington, DC, schedule, while they rejected Turbotrains? Both began service in 1969 as two parts of the same demonstration project. Probably because the Metroliners offered two things that the Turbotrain lacked, frequency and reliability. The Metroliners began service with six frequencies each way versus just two for Turbotrains. The air shuttles had pampered travelers with hourly departures based on their needs—no reservation necessary, just show up! There were just enough Metroliner frequencies to afford the traveler some flexibility. With but one Turbo in the morning and one in the evening, the Turbo traveler was locked in to the old *Bay State Limited* in the morning or the *Merchants Limited* in the evening service with only slower standard trains in between.

The Metroliners proved quite reliable, racing over the corridor's south end of 225 miles in under three hours and averaging seventy-five miles per hour. One trip each way was scheduled with one stop or no stops in two and a half hours at an amazing ninety-miles-per-hour average speed.

The Turbotrain featured lightweight cars, swiveling on one axle and missing first-class parlor cars. They broke down frequently. The Metroliners featured a first-class Metroclub car with food service at your seat. Both the Metroliners and the Turbotrain had to contend with deteriorated Penn Central track, forcing them to really race outside of the posted "slow orders." Both types of trains had difficulty meeting their 1969 schedules.

Congress Deals with the Twin Crises

By 1970, it was clear Congress would reluctantly have to deal with the passenger train crisis. In privately owned hands, they were quickly disappearing, and the majority of the American people were not ready for this. In 1970, Congress created the National Railroad Passenger Corporation or Amtrak, with plans to operate most inter-city trains. Purely commuter trains were excluded as they were subsidized separately by state agencies.

Amtrak began operating on May 1, 1971, inheriting a ragtag pool of engines and cars. While Congress had no problem with subsidy for highways, for commercial aviation, or for inland waterways, somehow they could not accept this for passenger trains. They needed to earn a profit or go out of business. Thus began a thirty-five-year congressional charade where our legislators pretended Amtrak could earn a profit "if the railroad were just run efficiently." Government was just the entity to do this!

In its first five years in the Boston–New York market, Amtrak did little differently. They struggled with the balky Turbotrain and fretted over its poor roadbed, owned by bankrupt Penn Central Railroad. With stability as their goal, the Boston–New York frequencies over the Shore Line never fell below eight or nine trips each way. Nor would they exceed ten trips each way. Other than with the Turbotrains, no speed records were attempted—just stability and survival.

1976—A Second Crisis Is Resolved

Federal money brought some badly needed new locomotives and cars to the aging Amtrak fleet. This capital infusion was not subsidy—just a way to help Amtrak reach self-sufficiency.

Federal money ended the question of whether there would be wholesale abandonment of northeast freight railroads. The federal government found a home for seven bankrupt railroads by creating Conrail, which began operations on March 1, 1976. Like Amtrak, Congress believed Conrail would be successful so the question of permanent subsidy need not come into play.

Since Conrail was created to be a freight railroad, a way had to be found to relieve it of passenger train burdens. This was done in two ways. Effective in 1976, Congress gave track ownership of most of the Northeast Corridor (Boston–Washington, DC) to Amtrak. In addition, Amtrak was assigned ownership of the hundred-mile Philadelphia–Harrisburg main line of the old Pennsylvania Railroad plus the sixty-two-mile New Haven–Springfield, Massachusetts, line of the old New Haven. Oddly enough, Congress withheld ownership of the fifty-six-mile Corridor segment from New Rochelle, New York, to New Haven, Connecticut, assigning ownership to Connecticut and New York transportation agencies that by 1983 would give this section of railroad a name—Metro-North Commuter Railroad. Between 1976 and 1983, Conrail would be the reluctant operator of this fifty-six-mile segment but was subsidized by the two state agencies for their efforts. This gave Metro-North Commuter Railroad time to get organized and take over. From the troubles and turmoil, a sea change had occurred. The Boston–New York rail corridor was now a public entity.

Some Early Amtrak Initiatives

As the 1980s dawned, Amtrak had succeeded in stabilizing the Boston–New York passenger service. Congress authorized monies to be set aside each year, beginning in 1976, with an act for the Northeast Corridor improvement. Roadbed deterioration ended and a better ride was on the way. New diesel locomotives and new straight electric engines came to Amtrak. The venerable electric engine, the GG-1, found its days were numbered. Straight electric engines began to run through from Washington, DC, to New Haven Connecticut, eliminating the Penn Station, New York, engine change. New Amfleet I passenger cars began to bump the older cars of former owners, the New Haven and the Pennsylvania Railroads.

In 1980, Amtrak was moving to concentrate its New York City service at Penn Station, rather than sharing traffic with Grand Central Terminal. More and more corridor trains were Boston–Washington, DC, run-throughs rather than Boston–New York City ones only.

In 1981, the erstwhile unthinkable happened! Amtrak placed all of its corridor trains on Hell Gate Bridge, pulling out of Grand Central Terminal. The only Amtrak trains remaining in Grand Central were the Empire Corridor trains to Albany and points beyond. Suddenly the FL-9 dual-purpose diesels with third-rail shoes for Grand Central were less needed. Many found a new home with Metro-North Commuter Railroad, who could use them for run-through service from Poughkeepsie and Danbury, eliminating engine changes or shuttles. Amtrak kept a few for Empire Corridor service.

Straight electric engines were back in the saddle again, and there was no further talk of de-electrifying the Stamford–New Haven main line. Turbotrain was gone by 1980, but there was now a record eleven Hell Gate Bridge Route trains each way. It took this trauma to end sixty-three years of underutilization.

By 1984, eight of the scheduled eleven trains over the bridge were bound for Boston. One was a purely New York-New Haven extension of a Washington–New York Metroliner. One was a Washington–Springfield run, and one was the resurrected Montrealor, operating from Washington, DC, to Montreal, Canada. The year 1980 also saw the revival of the Inland Route with through cars on one train each way between New York City and Boston via Springfield. This train would eventually be named the *Bay State* and had end-point cardings of an unremarkable five hours and forty-five minutes.

The New England Metroliners

By 1982, Amtrak had a solid success with its three-hour New York–Washington, DC, Metroliners, now on a *shuttle-competitive* hourly departure schedule from 6:00 a.m. to 7:00 p.m. The earlier multiple-unit electrics were being replaced with standard locomotives and cars. What could be done to beef up the corridor's north end, New York to Boston?

Amtrak introduced just two New England Metroliners (each way) in 1982. With consists limited to five cars plus a fast engine change in New Haven, Amtrak was able to reinstall a four-hour Boston–New York schedule, back where we were in 1949 to 1950 with the *Merchants Limited.* A premium fare was charged. This service lasted just two years, being withdrawn in 1984 for lack of business. Amtrak had learned once again (and after Turbotrain) that two fast trips each way were simply not enough to be shuttle competitive. From this point to 1994, our next "look-in" year, Boston–New York schedules reverted to nine or ten trips each weekday, with end-point times growing longer.

The 1994 Weekday Schedules

Via the Shore Line

New York		Boston	Boston		New York
7:01 am	Fast Mail	12:04 pm	6:00 am	New Eng. Exp.	10:14 am
9:30 am	Benjamin Franklin	2:33 pm	7:25 am	Mayflower	12:19 pm
11:30 am	Yankee Clipper	4:35 pm	9:05 am	New Eng. Exp.	1:15 pm
12:42 pm	New Eng. Exp.	4:55 pm	9:25 am	Minute Man	2:20 pm
1:35 pm	Patriot	6:53 pm	11:25 am	Yankee Clipper	4:21 pm
3:25 pm	Mayflower	8:23 pm	1:25 pm	Patriot	6:17 pm
4:55 pm	New Eng. Exp.	9:08 pm	3:30 pm	The Senator	8:25 pm
5:44 pm	The Senator	10:47 pm	4:30 pm	Merchants Ltd.	9:10 pm
7:25 pm	Merchants Limited	12:26 am	7:01 pm	Benj. Franklin	11:54 pm
3:15 am	Night Owl	8:39 am	10:20 pm	Night Owl	3:16 am

Via the Inland Route

New York		Boston	Boston		New York
11:30 am	Connecticut Yankee	5:15 pm	6:35 am	Conn. Yankee	12:19 pm
5:44 pm	Bay State	11:30 pm	12:25 pm	Bay State	6:17 pm

Shore Line Route Commentary

The good news was the increase since 1969 in frequencies from eight to ten trains each weekday. The long slide in frequencies had ended. The downside was the notable lengthening of end-point times. The four-and-a-half-hour average of 1969 had lengthened to five hours for most trains (illustrations 12-2 and 12-3). As if to show it could run fast if needed, two New England express departures each way managed to cover the 231 miles in as little as four hours and ten minutes. An extra fare was required to ride an express.

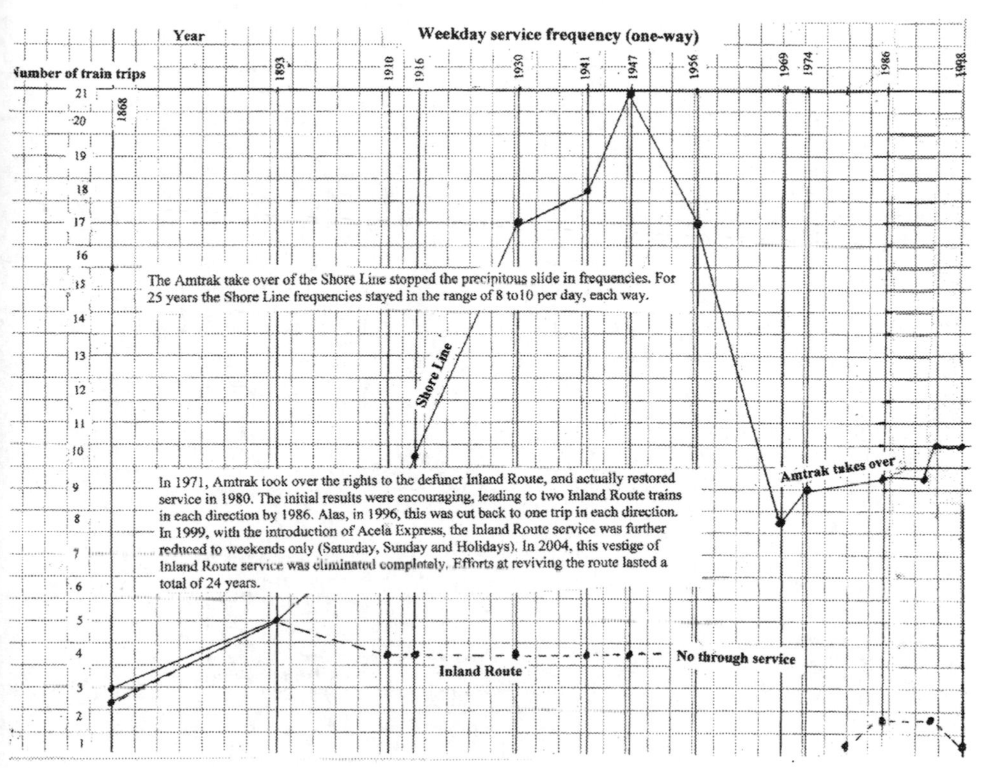

Year
Weekday service frequency (one-way)
Number of train trips
1868
1893
1910
1916
1930
1941
1947
1956
1969
1974
1986
1998
The Amtrak take over of the Shore Line stopped the precipitous slide in frequencies. For 25 years the Shore Line frequencies stayed in the range of 8 to10 per day, each way.
Shore Line
Amtrak takes over
In 1971, Amtrak took over the rights to the defunct Inland Route, and actually restored service in 1980. The initial results were encouraging, leading to two Inland Route trains in each direction by 1986. Alas, in 1996, this was cut back to one trip in each direction. In 1999, with the introduction of Acela Express, the Inland Route service was further reduced to weekends only (Saturday, Sunday and Holidays). In 2004, this vestige of Inland Route service was eliminated completely. Efforts at reviving the route lasted a total of 24 years.
No through service
Inland Route

12-2 Weekday service frequency to 1998

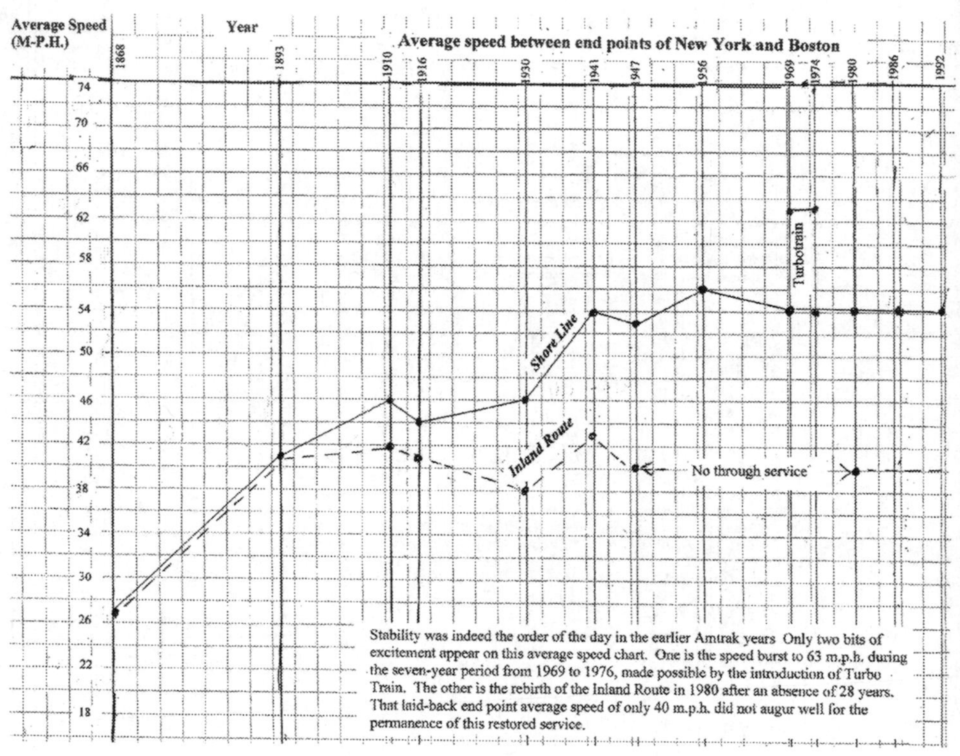

12-3 Average speed between end points of Boston and New York

Amtrak began to recognize the need for a train to arrive in New York before noon. A 6:00 a.m. express train broke the taboo of scheduling a train so early. Eastbound, Boston remained unreachable before noon from New York. Amtrak also began to recognize morning traffic was imbalanced, with the majority of travelers coming west from Boston. In the afternoon, this imbalance was reversed, favoring eastbound traffic from New York to Boston.

Each of the ten departures carried the name of a traditional train, some way out of their time-honored slots. The eastbound *Merchants Limited* left Penn Station for Boston at 7:25 p.m.

By 1994, the Boston–New York City passenger car fleet was generic—one train looked just like the next. Gone were special diners, parlor cars, or observation cars adorned with the name of their flyers. Besides, how many riders of 1994 associated *Merchants Limited*, *Yankee Clipper*, or *Patriot* with the panache of that former era? The time to drop the past came in 1995, when all trains became simply *Northeast Direct*. The glories and the cobwebs of the past were swept away. The above 1994 timetable would be the finale for the old names.

The fleet of night trains was completely gone by 1994. The one remaining night departure over the Boston–New York route carried only a sleeping car for Washington, DC, not even a set-out sleeper for New York City. Another era, that of overnight sleeping cars and overnight steamers in this market, was gone.

Inland Route Commentary

What began as a revival of the Inland Route with through Boston–New York City cars in 1980 had grown to two such trains by 1994. Amtrak was reaching out to Framingham and Worcester passengers, in particular.

The two through trains (no change of cars) were not truly solid trains. Both rode a Shore Line train between New York and New Haven, where the train was split with one proceeding via the Shore Line and the other via the Inland Route. The name assigned to the afternoon departure, the *Bay State*, was truly a route transformation of an old Shore Line flyer.

End point times averaged five hours and forty-five, setting no Inland Route records, yet just forty-five minutes slower than most of their Shore Line counterparts. Actually those ample end-point times reflected the downgrading of the once superb and double-tracked Inland Route. Conrail, the new owner of the ninety-eight-mile Boston–Springfield segment had singled almost fifty-five of these miles in 1987 and reduced the permitted top speed from seventy to sixty miles per hour. Amtrak, owner of the sixty-two-mile Springfield–New Haven segment had singled almost forty miles of their double track in 1992. Trains now had to contend with meets where the track was still doubled or a passing siding existed.

Market Share in 1994

Even with the modest increases in Boston–New York frequencies, Amtrak of 1994 could not exceed its old average of just 5 percent of all travelers making end-point journeys. Save for the two express trains, the leisurely five-hour schedules, so bold in 1910, did little to impress business travelers in 1994. Leisure travelers were attracted to the economy fares. Some of them were willing to get out of their automobiles and on to a train. To them, the train was a superior bargain to the pricier air shuttles or the cramped but economical buses.

In play in 1994 was a plan, as yet not fully funded or approved, to electrify the corridor from New Haven eastward 156 miles to Boston. Amtrak began a series of teaser ads urging the public to look forward to a new day in Boston–New York travel. Bullet-type trains would be used, and the run could be completed in about three hours. A new Penn Station would open in New York City, one utilizing space in the old postal service building, whose architecture mirrored the long-gone original Penn Station. A west-side connection was opened for Albany trains operating out of Penn Station and using an old freight line up the Hudson River to Spuyton Duyvil. With this, Amtrak completely vacated Grand Central Terminal, moving all trains to an increasingly congested Penn Station. The long buildup and launch of the Acela Express service is the subject of the next chapter.

Chapter 13: 1994 to Spring 2005

An Old Rail Line with the Promise of a Renaissance

By the year 1994, Amtrak, Congress, and the Coalition of Northeastern Governors had agreed on three major goals for Amtrak's Boston to New York line. The line would be fitted for high-speed service with end-point times of "about three hours." This move was intended to alleviate the need for a second land-eating and noisy Boston area airport. To help achieve these fast times, electrification would be completed between New Haven and Boston. In addition, a new high-speed train would be designed by Bombardier and Alstrom and modeled somewhat on the successful French TGV train that had racked up more than fifteen years of successful service.

Superimposing High Speed on an Existing Line

High-speed rail is usually defined as a line where trains can travel consistently at speeds of 125 miles per hour or faster. Curved track needs to be gradual, and grade crossings need to be eliminated. Some sovereign states that currently have high-speed rail have opted to dedicate a new right-of-way to these speedsters, thus not mixing freight trains and regional commuter trains with the fast trains. An exception is made on the approaches to large cities where existing rail lines are used at lower speeds. This exception is made because of the enormous land costs of trying to assemble a rail corridor in an existing and densely populated area. Once built, such a high-speed rail corridor provides far more consistent timekeeping and lower maintenance costs. However, the start-up costs are large even with the center cities exempted as noted above. This is the model used by Japan, Germany, Spain, China, South

Korea, and France. Other sovereign states have opted to superimpose their high-speed trains on existing rights of way, obviously a less costly solution but one with some drawbacks too. Realigning curves and closing old grade crossings in favor of overpasses or underpasses are costly too. The practical speed limit using the superimposing model is 125 to 150 miles per hour. Very high-speed trains (more than 150 miles per hour) invariably follow the dedicated right-of-way model. The superimposed or slower-speed model is followed by the United Kingdom and most of Italy. It is the model chosen by Amtrak, the governors' coalition, and Congress. We want high-speed rail, but we want it as cheaply as we can get it!

Three-Hour End-Point Times

For the past thirty-six years, Amtrak's Metroliners have been covering the 225-mile New York and Washington, DC, corridor in three hours. This has been a winning model, with service every hour from 5:00 a.m. through 8:00 p.m. Amtrak's share of the commercial market in this corridor is reported to be about 60 percent or more than any other single carrier, including air carriers or buses. Since New York-Boston is a corridor of almost identical length, it was only natural that the planners would settle on the three-hour figure as a worthy goal for the north end of the corridor to duplicate the proven achievements on the south end.

There are several problems with this comparison. The south end of the corridor is relatively flat with far fewer curves, bridges, and "slow orders" than there are on the northern stretch. In addition, Amtrak owns the entire south end but owns only 76 percent of the north end. On the south end, Amtrak sets the speed limits, and the various agency commuter trains comply. On fifty-six miles of the north end, a commuter railroad controls the speed limits (often seventy or eighty miles per hour), and Amtrak must comply. The northern-end commuter agency figures seventy to eighty miles per hour is just fine for it. If Amtrak wants a higher speed, let them fund it! This is currently not possible.

With 24 percent of their Boston–New York corridor speed restricted, it will be very difficult for Amtrak to achieve three-hour end-point times. The east of New Haven improvements have been considerable.

Electrification right through to Boston means faster acceleration and the elimination of time-consuming engine changes at New Haven. Superelevating the tracks has eased the passage through curves. Several short bursts of speed up to 150 miles per hour help reduce the New Haven to Boston former best time by a whopping thirty-eight minutes. These speed bursts are really teasing reminders of what we could have if we wanted to pay for it. Unfortunately, the New York to New Haven segment of this run is actually timed to take longer than it did in 1950! About five minutes is lost on this stretch.

A worse indignity awaits an Amtrak Acela Express train in the fifty-six-mile restricted area. Metro-North Railroad dispatches this stretch of track. The Metro-North dispatchers have the goal of keeping their own trains on time. After all, this is their railroad, and Amtrak is just a tenant. If the tenant keeps its trains on time and in their proper slot, there will be no Amtrak delay. However, just let them enter the trackage a few minutes late, and they could find themselves trapped behind a local train. Such a situation would have been unthinkable under the unified management of the old New Haven Railroad. Woe to the dispatcher who would further delay the late-running *Merchants Limited* by favoring a local train!

The Acela Express Is Introduced

In December 1999, the first few sets of the sleek new Acela trains were ready to enter service amidst high expectations (illustration 13-1). These high-speed train sets were initially carded at three hours and twenty minutes to cover the end points of Boston and New York. With the Acelas, could Amtrak boost its anemic commercial market share of 7 to 8 percent for the New York and Boston run? Could they hope to equal the 60 percent commercial share they had achieved on the corridor's south end? Would the comfort, the appeal of speed, frequency, and punctuality do the trick on the north end? Would the fare be competitive?

13-1 Acela Express #2031 at Boston South Station
Photo Das48

Teething Problems

Amtrak created false expectations for the Acelas. These trains were touted as the salvation to Amtrak's ridership and subsidy problems. These trains would enable Amtrak to turn the corner into solvency. Amtrak's political foes simply waited to see what the great introduction might produce in the way of negative political fodder. They were not disappointed! A nasty four-year legal dispute between Amtrak and the Acela's chief builder (Bombardier) ensued. The builder was suing Amtrak for making numerous and capricious changes to Acela's specifications and also for allowing its roadbed "to deteriorate." In turn, Amtrak was suing Bombardier for delivering a faulty product. Some of the initial faults were embarrassing and frivolous; others were more serious.

1. The pendulum used to stabilize the ride through curves could not swing out as far as proposed because of a lack of clearance.
2. The heavy spring tension of the pantograph was pulling down sections of the old "triangle" wire (between New Rochelle and New Haven).
3. Metro-North Railroad, the owner of this section of track, was replacing the old overhead wire with newer counterweighted wire, but replacing the entire fifty-six miles was scheduled to take ten years. Under the old triangle wire, Acela had its speed wings clipped to keep from pulling it down.
4. Some of the Acela's toilet doors would stick closed and locked, trapping passengers.
5. In August 2002, all Acelas were withdrawn from service for a week while cracks in brackets supporting the shock absorbers were repaired or replaced.
6. The builder was agonizingly slow in delivering the twenty trains sets, resulting in a very gradual buildup to the frequency required for true corridor service.
7. Because the new equipment was unreliable and subject to frequent breakdowns, no more than fourteen of the twenty sets could be placed in regular service. The balance had to be kept ready in case of breakdowns.

Infrastructure Problems

The magical three-hour end-point times for Boston–New York service has proven elusive for Amtrak. The old roadbed inherited from the former pace-setting New Haven Railroad had been upgraded but only partially. Full electrification all the way to Boston helped greatly. So did the improvements at Stamford Station, where four loading platforms had replaced the old bottleneck of only two platforms. The following infrastructure problems have yet to be fully addressed, as they will need to be if that three-hour schedule is to be realized.

1. The need for a flyover at New Rochelle Junction (Shell Tower), currently a place of chronic delays.
2. The need to complete the upgrading of the overhead wire on Metro-North Railroad to permit increased speeds.
3. Further upgrading of four movable bridges on Metro-North Railroad to eliminate slow orders.
4. Upgrading of Amtrak's three bridges, (1) over the Connecticut River at Old Saybrook, (2) the Niantic River at Niantic (completed in 2012), and (3) the Thames River at New London (completed in 2010).
5. Realigning three extremely sharp curves (with attendant speed restrictions) at Port Chester, Bridgeport, and New London.

The Acelas Are Positioned in the Market

As we entered 2004, Amtrak was well underway in positioning its premier trains in the marketplace. Even with its well-known flaws, Amtrak was able to place in service enough Acelas so that they could make eleven Boston–New York round trips each weekday. This plus nine regional trains making round trips each weekday brought the weekday one-way frequency to twenty trains (see illustration 13-2). Frequencies like this were last seen at the end of World War II when a record twenty-one trains plied the route each way. The average speed between end points climbed again to a record sixty-nine miles per hour (illustration 13-3). Following these illustrations is the 2004 schedule with a peak number of trains for recent times.

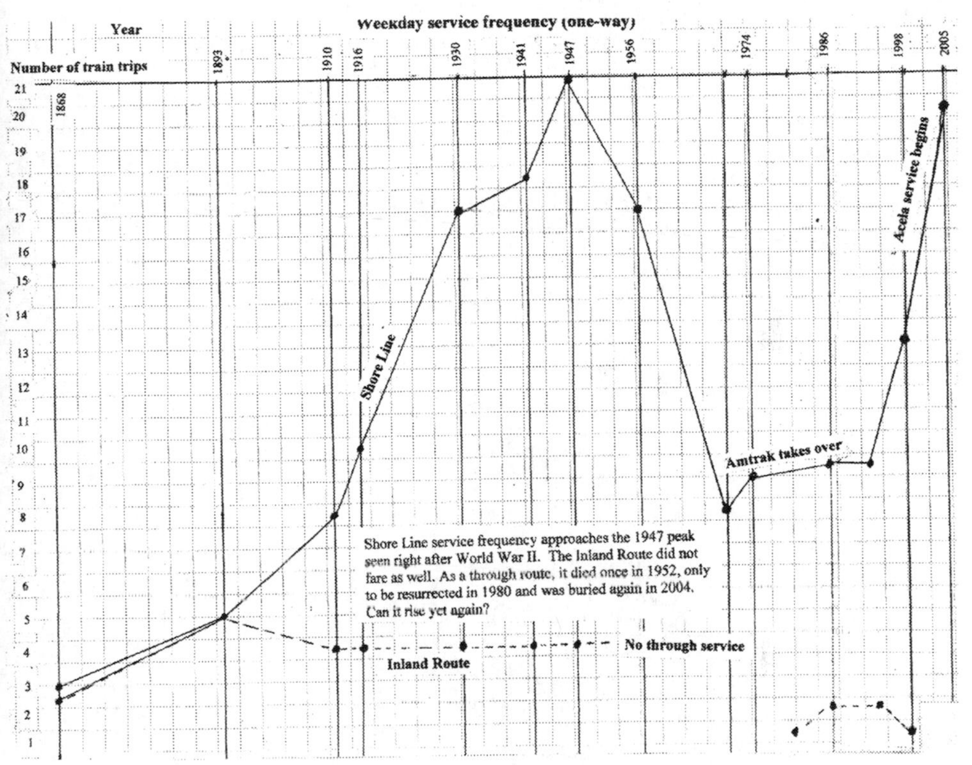

13-2 Weekday service frequency to 2005

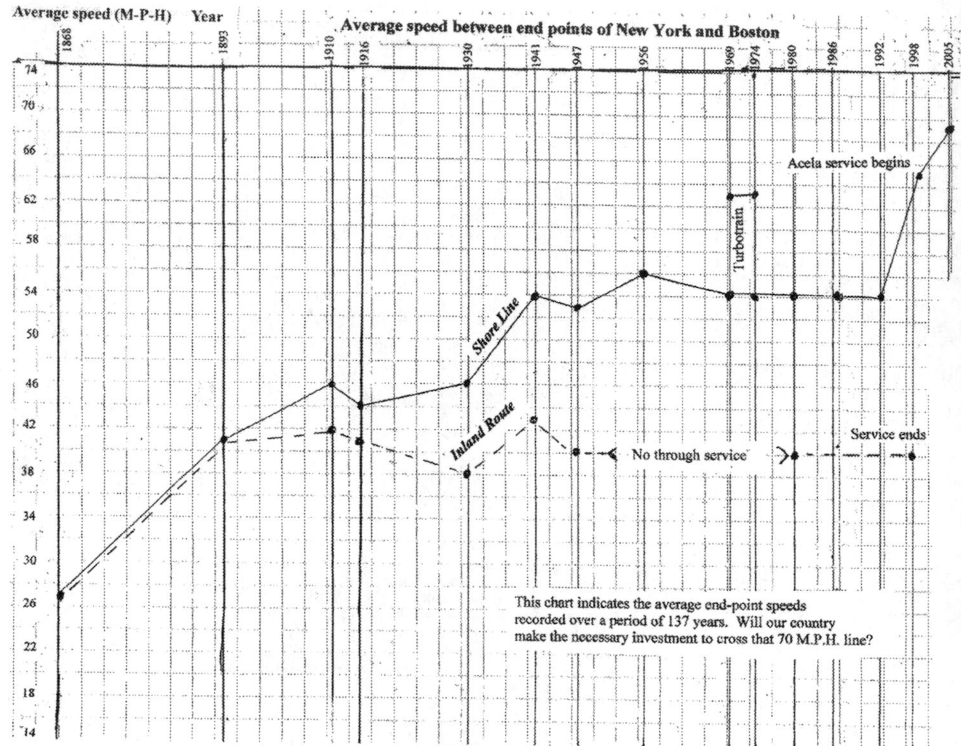

13-3 Average speed between end points of Boston and New York

2004 schedule with a peak number of trains for recent times

New York		**Boston**	**Boston**		**New York**
Eastbound			Westbound		
3:15 am	Regional	8:15 am	5:20 am	Acela	8:45 am
6:20 am	Acela	9:50 am	6:20 am	Acela	9:40 am
6:55 am	Regional	10:59 am	6:05 am	Regional	10:20 am
8:03 am	Acela	11:27 am	7:20 am	Acela	10:42 am
8:30 am	Regional	12:55 pm	8:20 am	Acela	11:45 am
9:03 am	Acela	12:26 pm	8:10 am	Regional	12:20 pm
10:03 am	Acela	1:27 pm	9:20 am	Acela	12:42 pm
11:00 am	Regional	3:15 pm	9:35 am	Regional	1:50 pm
12:03 pm	Acela	3:27 pm	11:20 am	Acela	2:42 pm
1:00 pm	Regional	5:10 pm	11:40 am	Regional	3:50 pm
2:00 pm	Regional	6:20 pm	1:20 pm	Acela	4:42 pm
3:03 pm	Acela	6:27 pm	1:40 pm	Regional	6:00 pm
3:30 pm	Regional	8:00 pm	3:20 pm	Acela	6:42 pm
4:00 pm	Acela	7:26 pm	3:10 pm	Regional	7:15 pm
5:00 pm	Acela	8:29 pm	4:20 pm	Acela	7:43 pm
5:40 pm	Regional	9:59 pm	5:20 pm	Acela	8:42 pm
6:00 pm	Acela	9:25 pm	5:35 pm	Regional	9:59 pm
7:00 pm	Acela	10:29 pm	6:20 pm	Acela	9:42 pm
7:30 pm	Regional	11:50 pm	7:25 pm	Regional	11:30 pm
8:00 pm	Acela	11:29 pm	9:45 pm	Regional	2:01 am

With this full schedule, Amtrak was attempting to attract the early morning New York to Boston traveler, getting such traveler to one of the three Boston area stations between 9:30 a.m. and 10:00 a.m., which was unprecedented in the history of this line. The above full schedule falls short of an hourly "memory" schedule as offered by the air carriers, but it comes close with the exception of a few midday holes. For punctuality, Amtrak's offerings were about as reliable as the air carriers. The weather dependent airlines were achieving an on-time rate of about 80 percent. Amtrak was unable to achieve any type of Swiss precision here, with delays built into its infrastructure and its equipment.

With the issues of frequency and punctuality addressed (as best as Amtrak could), the positioning of the Acelas continued by experimenting with fares. There was a day when a traveler could call the railroad station and ask, "What's the fare from New York to Boston?" Today, the answer, if you get to talk with a human voice, would be this: "That depends." Acela trains carry two classes of passengers, first class and business class. The regional trains also carry two classes of passengers, business class and coach class. In addition, all fares are subject to the day of the week variables plus the time of the day variables. There are fare variables for peak time, for shoulder time, and for regular or off-peak time. This bewildering business is known as *yield management*, first adopted by the airline industry to wring the last drop of profits from passengers, and Amtrak has now adopted it.

The adult fare from New York to Boston ranges from a low of $66.00 for off-peak coach travel on a regional train to as high as $149.00 for a peak-time first-class ride on Acela. Senior citizens enjoy a further 15 percent reduction, which is not valid on Acela trains. For $99.00, you can ride in Acela business class in peak times.

By way of comparison, consider the following fares for air travel and for bus travel:

Delta or US Airways Shuttle	peak time	$128.00
Greyhound or Peter Pan bus	all times	$35.00
Luxury Liner reserved seat bus	all times	$69.00

Business travelers are going to prefer the air shuttles or the Acela Express. Amtrak is keeping its business-class fares just below the air shuttle fare. The super-roomy first-class ride on Acela (with meals provided) is not available on the egalitarian air shuttles. Will the business-class Acela traveler trade a somewhat longer ride for more room and comfort at somewhat less cost? Amtrak is betting a sizeable number will.

For the leisure travelers, including seniors, students, and anyone traveling on a budget, Amtrak offers off-peak discounts. Even so,

Amtrak's off-peak fare of $66.00 will be beyond the reach of the most frugal. The luxury bus at $69.00 will appeal to some of the better-endowed travelers. The bargain fare of $35.00 (even less for some student fares) will have an exclusive market that Amtrak cannot touch.

These quoted fares are subject to constant change as the competitors jockey for their market share. New York to Boston is one of the most competitive markets in the entire country. Can Amtrak gain a 40 percent share in this environment? This is a tall order, yet Amtrak has several natural advantages.

The service is roomy and comfortable.
Parts of the trip are very scenic.
Most trips from Boston offer continuing service (without change) to Philadelphia, Wilmington, and Baltimore plus other Northeast corridor points. It is not just a Boston and New York service.

The Hell Gate Bridge Comes into Its Own at Last

When Amtrak implemented the above twenty trains each way schedule in 2004 plus two more exclusively for Springfield or north, the venerable structure at last began to realize its manifest destiny. This is bound to revive the question, "Did the Pennsylvania Railroad and the New Haven Railroad, joint owners of the bridge, permit their architect to overdesign the great structure?" With four tracks, two for passenger trains and two for freight trains, it has seemed so. For its first eighty-five years, this huge four-track structure has rarely seen more than a *total* (both ways) of twenty-six trains a day (sixteen passenger and ten freight). As freight trains no longer use this as a through Northeast Corridor route, the passenger-freight mix has changed. In 2005, there are forty-four scheduled weekday passenger train crossings and but two to four freight train crossings. The southern two tracks are energized and used chiefly by passenger trains. One of the two northern tracks has been removed, and the remaining track is de-energized. The remaining northern track can only be used by diesel-powered trains. Thus, the great structure could have been built for three tracks with no delay to freight traffic or as few as two tracks with minor freight traffic delays.

In defense of civil engineer and designer Gustav Lindenthal, how was he to know in 1910 that by 1980 almost all freight traffic would abandon the bridge? But is the final chapter written about the use of this bridge? Perhaps not! Politicians and transportation planners continue to talk about the need for that freight train tunnel under the Upper Harbor of New York City. If such a tunnel were to become a reality, the original northern two tracks over the great bridge could again pulse with freight traffic.

Brake Problems to Sideline All Acelas

On April 15, 2005, the great experiment using Acela trains to expand their Boston to New York market share ended abruptly. The disc brake rotors of some train sets had developed millimeter-sized cracks. For the sake of safety, all twenty Acela train sets were pulled from service. Officials were uncertain as to when the trains could be repaired and restored to service. The best guess was it would take three to four months to bring back the trouble-prone trains. After an absence of this length of time, Amtrak will need to gradually reintroduce the train. Will there be enough credibility to bring the customers back? Probably so. Oddly enough, everyone who has ridden an Acela train praises it for its beauty and its comfortable and fast ride. Only railroad officials seem to dislike it. These officials complain of its unreliability and its lack of flexibility. (Didn't we learn from the failed fixed-consist trains of the past, including Turbotrain, Roger Williams, the Dan'l Webster, John Quincy Adams, and the Comet?) Railroad officials complain the Acelas are grossly overpowered for the payload carried. Amtrak's president has made it clear he would never order any additional Acelas, although he might authorize the addition of several passenger cars to each consist.

How was Amtrak to react to the sudden absence of its premier service on the Northeast Corridor. This was emergency time!

The first decision was to try to protect that 40 percent market share on the corridor's south end. The Metroliners were resurrected with hourly departure schedules between New York City and Washington, DC. Every available piece of the older Amfleet cars were rounded up, sent Northeast, and pressed into immediate service. The trusty AEM-7 electric engines plus the newer HHP-8 engines would bear the brunt of the work.

Although not quite as fast as the Acelas, the Metroliner name was still well known to the public. The New York to Washington, DC, corridor, Amtrak's crown jewel, was to be protected as best it could and at all costs.

But what would happen to the Boston and New York section of the corridor? After all, wasn't the northern side of the corridor in a full renaissance with the Acelas as the centerpiece? Alas, this was all too true! But there simply was neither enough equipment nor engines available to even begin to try to replicate those eleven round-trip Acela trips. Amtrak reduced the twenty round trips to twelve round trips and identified two each way as Metroliners. Except for their brief and abortive efforts in 1983 (the New England Metroliners), the Metroliner name was scarcely a household name in New England. Here is the emergency schedule that was in effect in the spring of 2005 and presumably will be until the Acelas are reintroduced.

New York		Boston	Boston		New York
6:55 am	Regional	10:59 am	5:15 am	Regional	9:20 am
8:00 am	Regional	12:10 pm	6:00 am	Metroliner	9:45 am
10:00 am	Regional	2:15 pm	6:15 am	Regional	10:20 am
12:00 Noon	Regional	3:59 pm	6:55 am	Metroliner	10:45 am
2:00 pm	Regional	6:20 pm	8:20 am	Regional	12:15 pm
3:00 pm	Metroliner	6:45 pm	9:35 am	Regional	1:50 pm
4:00 pm	Regional	8:05 pm	11:40 am	Regional	3:50 pm
5:00 pm	Metroliner	8:49 pm	1:40 pm	Regional	6:00 pm
5:40 pm	Regional	9:45 pm	3:20 pm	Regional	7:15 pm
6:40 pm	Regional	10:40 pm	5:35 pm	Regional	9:50 pm
7:30 pm	Regional	11:50 pm	6:45 pm	Regional	10:40 pm
3:15 am	Regional	8:15 am	9:45 pm	Regional	2:01 am

The above lineup probably puts a temporary halt to any growth in market share. But it is a holding pattern that keeps the door (customer awareness) open until the premier trains are available once again. The above holding schedule temporarily "gives up" on delivering New Yorkers into Boston in time for a full workday. For business travelers requiring this earlier arrival, it is back to the air shuttles or a hotel in Boston the previous night. The night trains and the overnight boats are gone.

The Inland Corridor Disappears

With the Acelas stealing the limelight, few noticed that the Inland Route slipped quietly away. Here was the first through-train route between Boston and New York. Here was the route that served three major cities between Boston and New Haven versus only one city via the Shoreline. Here was the route that achieved parity with the Shoreline in 1893, both in service frequency and speed. It even matched the Shoreline with an all first-class (Parlor Car) train. It was a natural to be the favored corridor, but such was not to be.

The year 2004 was not the first time through service via the Inland Route died. Its first demise was in 1952 during the Budd Rail Diesel Car craze on the Boston and Albany. From 1952 to 1980 the Inland Route's demise would partially inconvenience Worcester passengers. Springfield would retain trains originating at that terminal. In 1952, the New Haven Railroad partially assuaged the Worcester rider's loss of through service by introducing rail diesel cars that shuttled between Worcester and New London (dubbed Shoreliners), where connections with Shoreline trains could be made. As the New Haven Railroad's financial fortunes declined in the late 1950s and early 1960s, so did the track on this long-branch line. Speed had to be reduced and end-point times lengthened. The railroad quietly buried the Shoreliners just before its 1969 merger with Penn Central Railroad.

The Inland Route remained dormant until Amtrak decided to revive the line in 1980. Initially Amtrak provided one round trip daily, and in 1986, they added a second round trip. The Boston and New York end-point times remained a laid-back 5 3/4 to 6 hours, enticing few travelers to try the route. Between 1987 and 1992, Conrail, then the owner of the old Boston and Albany, pulled out substantial sections of double track between Framingham and Springfield. Amtrak similarly single-tracked a substantial section of its Connecticut River line between New Haven and Springfield. The result of this downgrading was the need to add still more time to allow for the meets. In 1998, through daily Inland Route service ceased. However, for six more years Amtrak kept a weekend remnant in service. Finally in 2004, the second Inland Route death became official. With the Acelas racing between Boston and

New York in as little as three hours and twenty minutes, the five-hour Worcester to New York time became anachronistic. Worcester and Framingham passengers could take the expanded T (commuter rail) service into Boston and change to an Acela and equal or better the so-called through Inland Route time. Springfield passengers hardly noticed the "train of notice." They now had eight daily departures from Springfield to New York and points south on the corridor.

Will the Inland Route, like the phoenix, rise again for the third time? As traffic congestion increases along this corridor, another rebirth is possible.

The Last Word

This book chronicles the 170-year history of the Boston–New York commercial travel corridor. As a player in this commercial travel, rail passenger trains have had quite a ride! From humble origins in 1835, passenger trains rose to euphoric heights in the 1893–1910 period, when they enjoyed almost a complete hegemony, save for the overnight boats on Long Island Sound. After subsequent decades of prosperity, in the 1960s the passenger train operators plunged into deep despair. All passenger trains almost disappeared when at the last minute Amtrak came riding in to the rescue (with subsidies). After thirty years of operation (2001) Amtrak had succeeded in stopping the slide in commercial travel by rail, but market share was still anemic, humbled by their air and bus competitors.

Could Amtrak's Acela, the bullet train, help Amtrak recover a substantial market share in this intensely competitive market? This seems possible. Is Acela the right product to accomplish this? Can its flaws be fixed and its credibility restored? Here the jury is still out.

Chapter 14

An Assessment of How Our Country Perceives the Need for an Upgraded Rail Passenger Train System

How Well Is the Acela Doing (Boston and New York City) after Twelve Years of Operation?

A prolonged rollout of a faster Boston–New York rail service called Acela Express began in December of 1999. We are approaching the twelfth anniversary of this service. How is it doing?

On balance, the results are moderately positive. Here is a list of the achievements:

1. The weekday schedules of Acela Express (an all-first-class or business-class train, with no coach passengers carried) has settled in at ten trips each way with fewer trips on weekends.

2. Market share for all rail in this New England corridor (not just Acela) has climbed from 7 or 8 percent (before Acela) to 27 percent of all commercial trips. We obtained these figures by extrapolating from existing data.

3. End-point average timing is about three and a half hours or 69.5 miles per hour up from fifty-six miles per hour before Acela or the sixty-two miles per hour achieved during the seven years of Turbotrain operation (1969–1976).

4. The ridership of all trains (not just Acelas) in this corridor has increased.

5. Weekday frequencies (all trains) is now nineteen trains each way, up from ten trips each way before Acela.

6. Acela has attracted the time sensitive traveler back to riding the train. No more jokes about "you rode the *what?*"

7. Travelers like the ride on the Acelas. This contrasts sharply with the poor reception travelers gave to the lightweight trains of fifty-five years ago (see chapter 10).

Since the Boston–New York Acela was superimposed on a nineteenth-century roadbed and a commuter railroad regulates speed standards on one quarter of the entire line, costs were held down. Many a government official will tell you this Boston–New York improvement was the best we could do with the available money fifteen years ago. Nonetheless, the result is not really high-speed rail but more accurately higher-speed rail (than before). The naysayers will tell us the following:

1. Why have a 150-mile-per-hour segment tucked in the middle of the run that is barely fifteen miles long? Is this meant to be a teaser?

2. All this fuss and expense to achieve a paltry 7.5-mile-per-hour gain over the old Turbotrain record. Why did you bother?

3. If we have to spend billions to realize such small incremental gains, do we really need higher-speed rail in America? Instead, let's focus on more fuel-efficient cars and planes. They won't need major subsidies, and we can always drill for more oil as we need it.

4. You rail folks self-inflicted your own inhibitor to gaining more market share when in 1999 you eliminated unreserved coach seating. Now many people who used to just show up for the train, buy a ticket on the spot, and board the next unreserved train won't even try to get seats. The original and

successful Eastern Airlines Shuttle of 1962 didn't get its start by deliberately restricting seat availability.

Where Does the Boston Acela Go from Here?

The time-sensitive traveler will give up two and a half to three hours for a Boston–New York ride that is consistent, reliable, cost-competitive, and easy to access. The main problem facing the Boston Acela is about thirty to forty-five minutes of excess transit time, pushing it to the margins of full success. Amtrak discovered this in the 1980s in the New York–Washington, DC, segment of the corridor. During intense roadbed reconstruction, it was necessary to lengthen what was then called Metroliner schedules by about thirty minutes. Traffic immediately fell on the Metroliners. However, once three-hour schedules and even two-hour-and-forty-five-minute schedules were reintroduced, traffic bounced back.

Is it time to look again at the three-hour Boston–New York Acela as a possibility? What would it take to achieve this goal?

For every five minutes cut from the existing schedule, it would appear Amtrak would gain an additional 2 percent market share. Cut thirty minutes, and we take an existing 27 percent share and add another 12 percent for a total market share now at 39 percent. More equipment will be required. Hopefully enough could be made available to eliminate reserved seating in coaches as was the case for a period extending from 1850 to 1999—that's 149 years to prove it can be done!

Does America Need and Can It Afford High-Speed Rail?

Even if we define down the definition of high-speed rail to simply higher speed (than we have now), do we need it, and can we afford it? These are the two basic questions that have bedeviled this administration's efforts to launch an upgraded rail passenger system.

Most Americans were raised with the fly-drive model that has dominated the transportation scene for the last fifty years. If it's too far to drive, then fly! The rail alternative exists for perhaps 25 percent of our people who live in or near rail corridors, such as in the Northeast, California, or the Pacific Northwest. Most of the remaining 75 percent of our citizens have never been on a train! It would be a new learning experience to even attempt a train trip.

The temptation is to stay with what you know. The family car and commercial aviation is all we have known and perhaps all we will ever need. Why not just build more roads and keep the fifty-year model? Under even the most optimistic of rail scenarios, more roads can and will be constructed (or reconstructed). Still, even automobile advocates will admit the old model is beginning to fray. It is becoming increasingly difficult to maintain the road infrastructure for a growing population where each adult aspires to own his or her own personal transportation. It is becoming increasingly difficult to keep the gas tanks filled for our 6 percent of the world's population who currently consume 25 percent of the world's fuel. As the standard of living of much of the developing world (as in China, India, Brazil, Africa) rises and these countries increase their consumption of oil products, can we afford the increased price competition for limited world supplies? Would it not be prudent to prepare the way for an alternative? How high must the per-gallon price of fuel rise before some alternatives to the model begin to make sense?

If we begin to develop rail passenger corridors, will these corridors be genuine high-speed corridors, or will compromise again force the sharing of the right-of-way with slower freight and commuter trains? How much are we willing to invest in the rail alternative, and how fast must we have a full payback? As yet we don't have a clear vision of where we need to go.

Three of the states that initially received some federal funding to begin planning for high-speed rails have refused or returned their federal funds (Wisconsin, Ohio, and Florida). Was this a rejection of high-speed rail based on costs and potential liabilities? Or is it a clear statement of the lack of an apparent need? Other states have accepted federal funds and are now pushing ahead with their planning. With no national consensus, how can a national system evolve? Is one even necessary?

The Utilization of the Hell Gate Bridge

Since the introduction of this topic in chapter 7, we continue to be amazed at the size, cost, and capacity of this most arresting capital investment—a structure that will soon celebrate its hundredth anniversary.

The building of the Hell Gate Bridge and its seven miles of a connecting railroad to join the New Haven Railroad and the Pennsylvania Railroad was such a massive and costly project that it has caused naysayers to point to it as a loser for its first sixty-four years. As proof, they cite that rail traffic over the bridge never exceeded twenty scheduled passenger trains (in both directions) and twelve freight train movements from its inception in 1917 until 1981.Worse yet, the bridge was built with a total of four tracks, two for passenger and two for freight. Talk about overbuilding!

But wait! That utilization picture has been changing and improving. After 1981 when Amtrak moved all of their Boston–New York City trains to the Hell Gate Bridge and Penn Station, withdrawing from Grand Central Terminal, the bridge became a busier place. Meanwhile, the freight train operator, Conrail, successor to the New Haven and the Pennsylvania Railroads' freight operations, all but abandoned Bay Ridge, Brooklyn, thus relegating freight operations over the Hell Gate Bridge to locals for Long Island. Twelve freight trains crossing the great bridge now became just two to four trains daily. The net effect of this change was a major increase in passenger train frequency but the loss of most of the through freight business.

For the next eighteen years (1981–1999) the bridge resonated to ten passenger trains in each direction and one or two freight movements. With the introduction of the Acela beginning in 1999, the bridge currently hosts twenty-one passenger trains in each direction plus the residual freight trains.

Still more train moves are coming. In August of 2016, the Sunnyside–Grand Central Terminal link of the Long Island Railroad is scheduled to open with up to thirty Long Island Railroad trains operating directly into Grand Central Terminal (instead of Penn Station). This will have the effect of freeing up some platform slots at Penn Station for use by New Jersey Transit and some Metro-North New Haven Line commuter trains that now exclusively serve Grand Central Terminal. These Metro-North Line trains will leave the main line at New Rochelle Junction (Shell) and move down the current Amtrak route over Hell Gate Bridge and into Penn Station, New York City. The new commuter cars, dubbed M-8s, will have multiple electrical collection systems, including pantographs for overhead wire and third-rail shoes that collect power by overriding a third rail (as in the approach to Penn Station) as well as under riding a third rail (as is the present practice in approaching Grand Central Terminal).

Thus, by 2016 when construction is complete, the Hell Gate Bridge could host as many as of forty passenger trains each way plus a few freight trains. The great bridge was built for precisely this level of traffic, even though it will have taken a hundred years to achieve this level of traffic. In truth, the Hell Gate Bridge is nowhere near being maxed out.

Metro-North Railroad has the advantage here with its access via the Hell Gate Bridge wide open. New Jersey Transit has just the opposite problem with its Hudson River access nearly at capacity and with its plans for additional access (access to the Region's Core) recently blocked by order of the New Jersey governor.

14-1 Acela at Old Saybrook, Connecticut
Photo by Michael Kurras
Credit goes to Shreder 9100

An image of an Amtrak Acela Express as it is running through Old Saybrook, Connecticut.

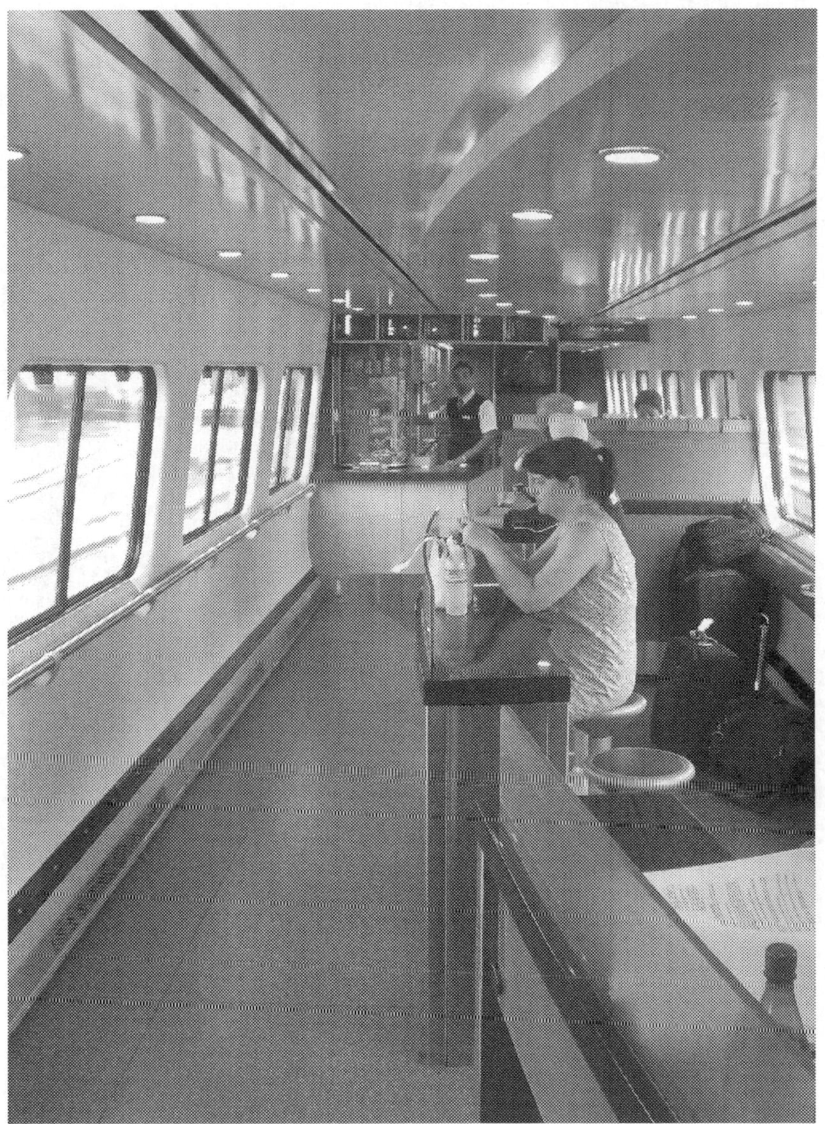

14-2 Acela Express cafe car interior
Photo by Daniel Case

14-3 Acela Express business coach
Photo by Nicholas Stambach

At Baltimore Penn Station.

14-4 Acela Express crossing the Susquehanna River
Photo by James G. Howes

Southbound train at Havre de Grace, Maryland.

14-5 Acela on Randalls Island Causeway
Photo by Jim Henderson

Looking east as a southbound train on the Randalls Island Causeway turns east to cross Hell Gate Bridge.

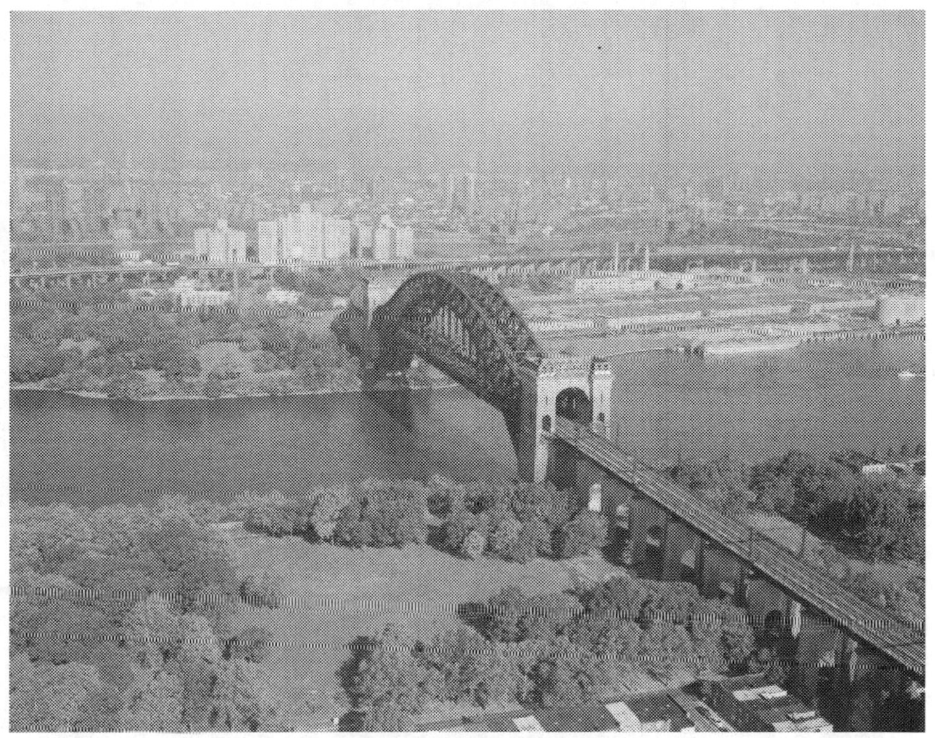

14-6 Hell Gate Bridge
Photo by Jet Lowe

Hell Gate Bridge spanning East River, Ward's Island, and Astoria, New York. From west looking northeast, with Queens in the foreground.

14-7 Overhead view of Acela Express
Credit goes to SignalPAD, Derek Yu

Acela Express power car hums past a Forest Hills bound MBTA Orange Line train. Photo was taken from an overpass between Massachusetts Avenue and Ruggles.

14-8 Three Acelas
Photo by Braditude

Three parked Acela trains in South Station, Boston.

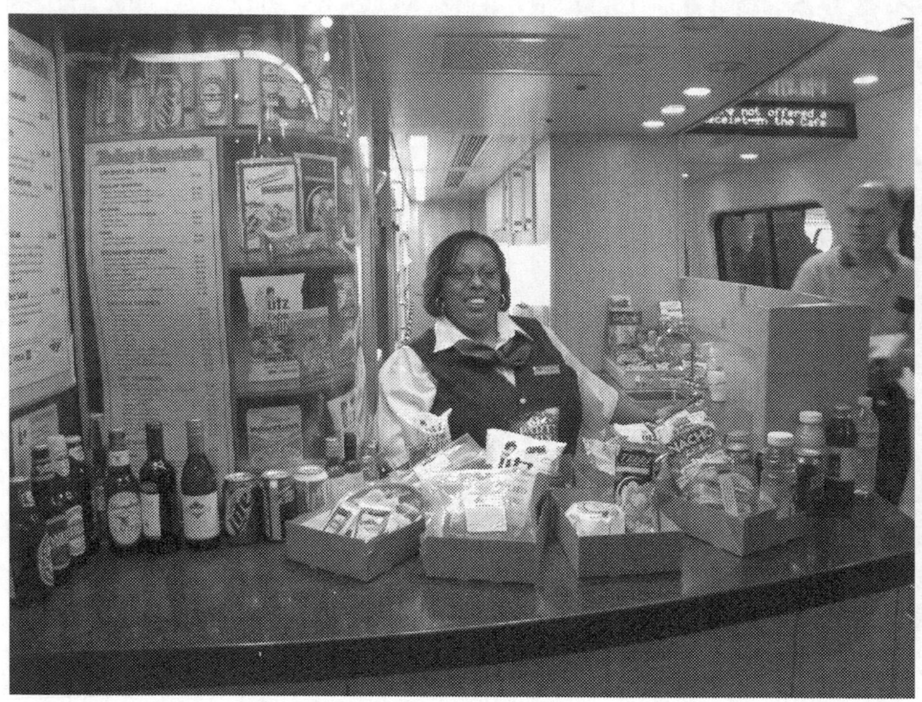

14-9 Acela Express cafe car choices
Photo by Ben Schumin

14-10 Acela at Kingston Station
Photo by Daniel Case

Passing through Kingston Station, Rhode Island.

14-11 Acela at Ninth Avenue
Photo by Jim Henderson

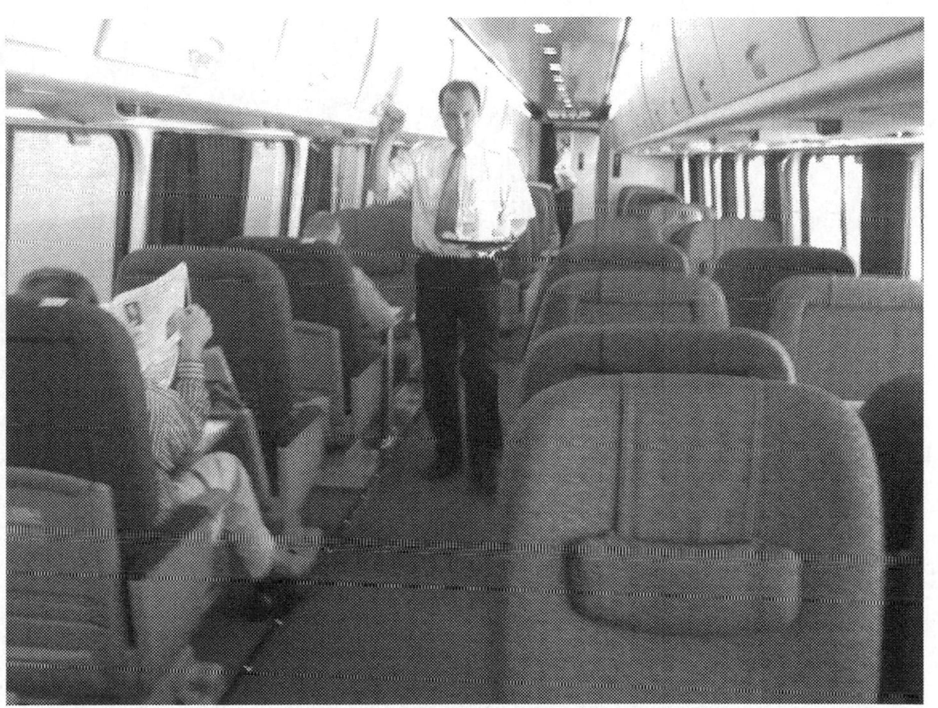

14-12 First-class car on an Acela Express
Photo by Len Edgerly

Resources

Alter, J. Cecil. *Early Utah Journalism.* Salt Lake City: Utah State Historical Society, 1938.

Arcara, Roger. *Westchester's Forgotten Railway: An Account of the New York, Westchester and Boston Railway Company.* New York: Quadrant Press, 1962.

Ball, Don Jr. *America's Colorful Railroads.* Danbury, NH: Reed Books, 1978.

Baxter, Raymond J., and Arthur G. Adams. *Railroad Ferries of the Hudson and Stories of a Deckhand.* New York: Fordham University Press, 1999.

Beebe, Lucius, and Charles Clegg. *The Trains We Rode.* New York: Promontory Press, 1993.

Cudahy, Brian J. *Rails under the Mighty Hudson.* Bratleboro, VT: The Stephen Greene Press, 1975.

Doughty, Geoffrey H. *New Haven in Color, Volume 1.* Scotch Plains, NJ: Morning Sun Books, 2003.

Hubbard, Freeman. *Encyclopedia of North American Railroading.* New York: McGraw-Hill, 1981.

Hungerford, Edward, *Locomotives on Parade.* New York: Thomas Y. Crowell Co., 1940.

Jacobs, Timothy. *The History of the Pennsylvania Railroad.* Greenwich, CT: Bison Books, 1988.

Jensen, Oliver. *The American Heritage History of Railroads in America.* New York: American Heritage Publishing Company, a subsidiary of McGraw-Hill, 1975.

Klein, Aaron E. *The History of the New York Central System.* Greenwich, CT: Bison Books, 1985.

Lynch, Peter E. *New Haven Railroad.* St. Paul, MN: MBI Publishing Company, 2003.

Porter, Horace. *Railway Passenger Travel.* Scotia, NY: Americana Review, 1888.

Public Timetables of the New York, New Haven and Hartford Railroad, The New York Central System, and the New York and New England Railroad and Predecessors and Successors, including Amtrak for the Years 1868, 1869, 1870, 1893, 1905, 1916, 1930, 1937, 1941, 1947, 1956, 1966, 1972, 1981, 1988, 1998, 2005, and 2011.

Salsbury, Stephen. *No Way to Run a Railroad: The Untold Story of the Penn Central Crisis.* New York: McGraw-Hill, 1982.

Swanberg, J. W. *New Haven Power.* Medina, OH: Alvin F. Stauffer, 1988.

Warner, Sam B. *Streetcar Suburbs: The Process of Growth in Boston 1870–1900.* Cambridge, MA: The President and Fellows of Harvard College, 1962.

White, John H. *The American Railroad Passenger Car, Part One.* Baltimore, MD: The Johns Hopkins University Press, 1978.

White, John H. *The American Railroad Passenger Car, Part Two.* Baltimore, MD: The Johns Hopkins University Press, 1978.

Ziel, Ron. *The Long Island Railroad in Early Photographs.* New York: Dover Publications, 1990.

Index

C

D

E

F

H

I

J

N

O